Change Competence

Organizations are often forced to change and adapt as a result of internal or external circumstances—whether the impetus is vision and ambition, a competing organization, societal pressure, or financial pressure. In this book, the authors posit that successful change requires the coherence of five elements: Rationale and Effect, Focus and Energy, and Connection.

In *Change Competence*, they present a vision of change management centered around these five elements, along with a model and method for diagnosing, approaching, and developing change management in a purposeful way. The book demonstrates the nuances and applications of the Change Competence Model with the use of a single integrated case, from identifying elements ripe for change, to coping with barriers, to varying approaches to change, to the different leadership roles that emerge in relation to the five key elements of change management.

This book will be of interest to practitioners and students in change management, organizational behavior, and organizational development.

Steven ten Have, Ph.D., is full Professor of Strategy and Change at the VU University Amsterdam, the Netherlands, visiting professor at the Nyenrode Business University, the Netherlands, and Partner at TEN HAVE Change Management.

Wouter D. ten Have, Ph.D., is University Lecturer of Organization and Change at the VU University Amsterdam, the Netherlands, visiting University Lecturer of Change Management (MBA Healthcare Management) at the Amsterdam Business School, the Netherlands, and Partner at TEN HAVE Change Management.

Anne-Bregje Huijsmans, MSc, is Consultant at TEN HAVE Change Management.

Niels van der Eng, MSc, Ph.D. candidate, is University Lecturer of Organization and Change at the VU University Amsterdam, the Netherlands, Head of Research, and Consultant at TEN HAVE Change Management.

Routledge Studies in Organizational Change & Development

Change Competence
Implementing Effective Change

**Steven ten Have,
Wouter ten Have,
Anne-Bregje Huijsmans and
Niels van der Eng**

Routledge
Taylor & Francis Group

LONDON AND NEW YORK

First published 2015
by Routledge

2 Park Square, Milton Park, Abingdon, Oxfordshire OX14 4RN
711 Third Avenue, New York, NY 10017

Routledge is an imprint of the Taylor & Francis Group, an informa business

First issued in paperback 2018

Library of Congress Cataloging-in-Publication Data
Have, Steven ten.
    Change competence : implementing effective change / by Steven ten Have, Wouter ten Have, Anne-Bregje Huijsmans, Niels van der Eng. — 1 Edition.
        pages cm. — (Routledge studies in organizational change & development ; 9)
    Includes bibliographical references and index.
    1. Organizational change.   2. Leadership.   3. Organizational effectiveness.   I. Title.
    HD58.8.H388 2015
    658.4'06—dc23
    2014035438

ISBN: 978-1-138-81861-3 (hbk)
ISBN: 978-1-138-61691-2 (pbk)

Typeset in Sabon
by Apex CoVantage, LLC

This book is the translated version of the Dutch book *Veranderkracht – Succesvol doelen realiseren*. If due to the translation process certain sentences fully match the original English work from which they are adapted, this was purely accidental and unintentional. Where indicated we shall revise them.

Translation: House of Words, www.houseofwords.nl

www.changecompetence.com

Contents

Figures

Tables

1 Change Competence

Managers frequently struggle with formulating a good strategy and direction for their organizations. It is often difficult to choose and prioritize, as the case in Chapter 7 shows. Everything needs to be done and everything seems important. This is also referred to as priority proliferation. It also often seems hard to translate a chosen strategy or direction into a vision for change, into a story that rings true and that motivates. A good strategy and change vision is a start. A good start is half the job: no less, but also no more. This must be followed by accomplishments, by results. This is often when it becomes clear that managers have problems in successfully converting their plans to results. The story from Chapter 7 about the chairman and Anne attests to this. Such problems are often rooted in the inability to flesh out the necessary change process; the capacity for change is lacking or inadequate. An effective change process stands or falls by an organization's change competence.

WHY DOES CHANGE NEED TO BE IMPROVED?

Dying Organizations

The average lifespan of an organization has declined over the last two decades from 20 to 12.5 years.[1] Organizations disappear primarily because when facing changing circumstances they adapt incorrectly, too much, unnecessarily, or not at all. The photography chain Kral went bankrupt by clinging too long to analog photography, despite the emergence of the digital camera. Eastman Kodak brought the photo camera into almost every American household, but the company switched over from analog to digital too late. When the world was already 'digitalizing,' Kodak was still making major commitments to the sale of old-fashioned cameras in China and India—emerging markets where the sale of those cameras plummeted as quickly as in the United States. Various publishing houses also saw the shift to a digital world too late. Their strong commitments to printed media ensured that many publishers missed the 'digital boat' and had to pull out all the stops not to fall too far behind.

Failing Changes

A stubbornly held opinion in both theory as well as practice is that 70% of all changes fail.[2] It is a belief that is 'happily' turned to within the context of 'managing expectations,' 'explaining' actual failure or the introduction of a new concept that looks sure to succeed. First off, methodological caveats can be placed on the 70% and similar percentages. Looking more meticulously helps. To what kind of change do these percentages pertain? For example, failure percentages appear to differ. Research[3] shows that cultural change fails in 80% of the cases (although it should be noted that this type of change seems more difficult to measure). More straightforward changes, such as cost reductions or the redesign of operating processes, succeed more often than fail. In those cases, the failure rates are around 35%. Nevertheless, practice indeed shows that there is still much room for improvement in the change process.

Faltering Execution

Many managers experience the relationship between plan and execution (i.e., strategy and implementation) to be problematic. This is often due to a lack of understanding of and insight into the process that needs be bridged between the stated goal and the realization of that goal.[4] This problem is also called the implementation gap or the execution factor.[5] According to the previously cited study, strategy implementation fails in 42% of the cases. Mankins and Steele[6] estimate this strategy-to-performance gap to be 37% (see Figure 1.1).

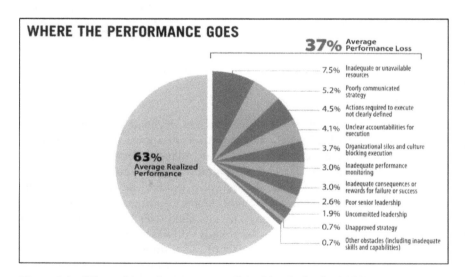

Figure 1.1   Where the performance goes (Mankins & Steele, 2005)

The chart shows the average performance loss implied by the importance ratings that managers in the survey of Mankins and Steele gave to specific breakdowns in the planning and execution process (p. 68).

The meaning of these failure percentages associated with the change and implementation processes can be put into perspective at macro level. Ultimately, it comes down to the question whether there are enough organizations that do have success and survive. But every failed or non-optimal change is one too many. The consequences in terms of public and social costs, waste of human capital, social unrest and collective lack of confidence should not be underestimated. Even if much succeeds, the question must be asked if there are not too many unnecessary failures, whether it can be improved. Are the interests and rights to exist of individual organizations, their employees, other stakeholders and scarce resources handled with care?

Aside from this, there are examples of successful changes that show what the realization of ambitions does to people and organizations. Examples where not only organizational goals are achieved, but where energy and development at an individual level also receive an impulse. What must happen for this to occur more often?

Purposive Change

Many insights and ideas about change get hung up in notions about dynamics and elusiveness. Such notions fall short when dealing with a perspective in which responsibility and getting something done and implementing it (regardless how difficult or obstinate the topic or circumstances may be) are central. As Bower[7] says: "It is one thing to recognize that a corporation is a complex non-linear system interacting with a very rich and changing environment. It is another to provide a map of that system that permits managers to act in an intentionally rational fashion."

Purposive change (intentional change) stands for goal-oriented, goal-conscious and efficient change, having the mission, its right to exist or the aim of the organization as its basis. This type of change concerns changing with a specific purpose or with an explicit intent: usually, this is the (improved) realization of organizational goals. Efforts are guided by a higher purpose, energy is consciously focused on that purpose and it is ideally done as efficiently as possible. Where possible, purposive or intentional specifically means that the effort is well thought out and guided by the organization's mission. It must especially provide a counterweight to a lack of professionalism, to rashness and to unnecessary experimentation at the expense of the future and the continuity of the organization, of the well-being of employees and the prosperity of customers and other stakeholders. Intentional, however, does not mean that spontaneous change, personal initiative or self-management is not taken into account or isn't used. On the contrary, intentional change demands, through a bottom-up initiative, for example, consciously providing room to experiment and improvisation as an alternative to the forms of management and direction that might be counterproductive in that situation.

Purposive change revolves around the link between idea and realization, or plan and execution: respectively, *what it should be* and *how it should be accomplished*. Many organizations and managers struggle with this combination. At times the plan is too big and overwhelming, whereby the organization does not have the body to be able to bear the change. The necessary change capacity is lacking. In other cases, there is ample energy and willingness to change, but a common goal, vision or direction is lacking. Often there is the necessary ambition or need, but there's a lack of coordination and cohesion. This results in a flow of fragmented and often conflicting, or at least confusing and wasteful change initiatives.

What is missing in such situations is a fruitful connection between the plan and the execution. Bower[8] posits, "If we understand that purposive change in a complex system means that most things are connected, then what we need is research that directly deals with those problems (multidisciplinary, non-linear dynamic system)." In complex systems such as organizations, most is directly or indirectly connected. This is why it is remarkable that organizational changes are never or rarely approached in this way. Instead, fragmentation and lack of cohesion between various components and change initiatives are the rule rather than the exception. For Bower's purposive change to become a reality, a bridge must be built between *what it should be* and *how it should be accomplished*; between plan and execution. In diagram form this is:

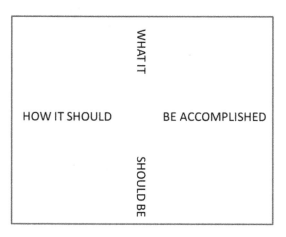

Figure 1.2   Bower's purposive change: 'what it should be' (the plan) and 'how it should be accomplished' (the execution)

Purposive change involves goal-oriented, goal-conscious and effective change. In this light, *what it should be* (the plan) is at the service of the mission and the organization is the instrument by which the mission is to be realized. When adapting the organization, it is sometimes unclear how the change contributes to the mission. Preferences of individual managers or what is fashionable may then seem more determinant for actions and interventions than that what is actually needed. The starting point of a change must be logical and appealing, and not only to the organization: it is also important for individual employees and specific groups that they see and 'feel' the reason to change. If not, cynicism, lack of understanding, counter-productivity and self-interest will largely prevail.

CHANGE VISION—WHAT IT SHOULD BE

A good start of an intentional change demands a vision of the actual situation and a clear story. This is necessary in order to have what is desirable or necessary get done, that otherwise will not get done. This involves both the highest and the lowest level relevant to the change, and everything in between. A change vision must combine an ambition at the organizational level with a translation for specific individuals and groups. A larger story (the Rationale) and a smaller story (the Effect) put together will form the change vision. In this light, the change vision can be described as the ability of an organization to continually identify opportunities and threats in its environment, and to successfully translate these into changes for the organization.

Rationale—The Larger Story of Change

The Rationale is the idea behind the change. The vision and logic on which the change is based. It is the reason for change, and it must 'ring true' not only in a logical and rational sense: the change must also be 'appealing,' in instinctive and emotional terms. The Rationale stands for the *why* of the change, the big picture, the 'larger story.'

Effect—The Smaller Story of Change

The other part of the change vision is the Effect. If the Rationale stands for the larger story, the Effect forms the smaller story of the change. Effect is concerned with the concrete, desired and undesired consequences of the change in terms of results, costs and yields, feelings and perceptions. This especially applies to individual stakeholders and specific groups that play a role in the change or which are affected by the change.

As a combination, the Rationale with the larger story and the Effect with the smaller story can be seen as Bower's *what it should be*. It shows how 'it' should be, and particularly the motives behind it. It is in the combination of the Rationale and the Effect from which the vision for change must be made clear.

CHANGE CAPACITY—HOW IT SHOULD BE ACCOMPLISHED

The change capacity must be up to the task, in order to be able to fulfill the change vision. Change capacity translates into the capacity of an organization to adapt to changed and changing circumstances. Focus and Energy—the constituent elements of change capacity—must both individually and combined make it possible to realize the change. Focus stands for the frameworks within which the desired behavior, the direction, is expressed and directed. Energy is the fuel for the change. People and means, inspiration and budget, leadership and professional autonomy. Energy without Focus turns an organization into a 'chicken with its head cut off.' Focus without Energy leads to an anemic organization that functions mechanically at best.

Focus—The Direction of the Change

Focus stands for the direction of movement. The Rationale or *motivation* for movement must be converted to a *direction* of the movement. For those who need to contribute to the change, it is not enough just to see *that* something needs to change. To be able to contribute, it must also be clear and tangible *what* exactly has to change and *how*. Behavioral frameworks, in the form of clear strategic choices, structures and systems, priorities, exemplary behavior and task descriptions, must provide the direction of movement.

Energy—The Ability to Change

Adjustments of the organization are often necessary for the realization of the change vision; new frameworks must be created. In addition, the vision must be brought to life by the change changeability of the organization. This ability involves the synthesis between the preparedness and readiness of employees, that in combination with leadership and availability of resources partly determine the attainability of the change.

Preparedness has to do with the willingness of employees; readiness as to the question of whether they are sufficiently equipped (do they possess the right knowledge, skills and experience) for the change and the new situation. Sometimes employees are willing to support a change (high preparedness), but feel unequipped or insufficiently equipped (low readiness). The reverse happens as well; this is often perceived as a form of resistance. The two axes form the following quadrants:

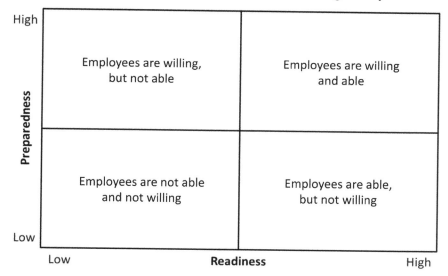

Figure 1.3 Preparedness versus readiness

The combination of Focus and Energy is expressed in the second section of Bower's purposive change: *how it should be accomplished*. It is this combination that reflects the change capacity of the organization and provides insight into what is needed to realize the change vision, i.e., *what it should be*, in terms of frameworks (to create a clear direction for change) and in terms of capacity (to start and continue that movement).

CONNECTION—THE CATALYST

Connection is the fifth factor, essential for the individual and combined action of the other factors: a catalyst. Connection ensures the cohesion and alignment between the other four determining factors (Rationale, Effect, Focus and Energy) by steering using the goals and strategy for change, but also by being in reciprocal contact as involved parties. Leadership, both formal and informal, plays a key role in this process. What is important is knowing what is taking place and how it is (really) going. Keeping a finger on the pulse, and having a good field of view, a helicopter view. But it is not only oversight and insight that are important. It also means being able to work together and to have all involved parties and factors cooperate. Connection ensures that all this 'balances' and 'works' by integrating and translating, signaling and influencing and by providing cohesiveness; in terms of content and socially, methodically and emotionally.

THE CHANGE COMPETENCE MODEL—SYMBOL OF CHANGE

The five factors (Rationale, Effect, Focus, Energy and Connection) must always work in conjunction. They cannot function without each other, and the design of one has consequences for the functioning of the other. The lemniscate (symbol of infinity) has been chosen as the shape and symbol to reflect and emphasize that connection between the five concepts. This is apt, since thinking in terms of a lemniscate entails continuously returning movements instead of linear lines. The thought process is shaped by rhythms, and less so by phases; the process is like:

- an inductive-deductive rhythm between facts and thoughts;
- an ethical-practical rhythm between goals and methods;
- an investigative-executive rhythm between insights and decisions;
- a speaking-acting rhythm between words and actions.

The lemniscate shape bears an intrinsic dynamic component. The shape is apt for the topic of change. The lemniscate has no specific start point or end point, which consequently supports circular causality thinking.[9] When seen in this light, a change is action as well as reaction and cause as well as result. The lemniscate as a shape is also associated with a symbolism that is useful when thinking about change. It offers points of departure for using metaphors and other forms of imaging to clarify issues that often can't be conveyed (well) through 'standard language.'

The uninterrupted lines, without start and end point, can be equated, for example, to the iterative process that characterizes many changes. Change is often a search process for what works and what does not work, in the case of the latter, a return to 'the drawing board' is necessary. This is not, by the way, a license to choose a trial-and-error approach over an approach that is well-thought-out in advance; it 'only' shows that no matter how well-thought-out a change process can be, it is wise to continuously monitor the results to verify they are keeping up with the expectation. If the latter is not the case, adjustments must be made.

The five factors and their mutual interconnectivity can be shown through two lemniscates and a connecting circle, a magnification of the essential midpoint or the connection. This creates the Change Competence Model (see Figure 1.4).

The Vertical Lemniscate—The Upright-Standing Eight

The Greek word lemniscate means flower garland. The upper loop of this decoration would go around the head, the lower loop around the lower part of the body, the abdomen. The garland crosses at the level of the heart. It also depicts the number 8, which in numerology is symbolic for harmony, totality and completeness. In Chinese tradition, the number 8 stands for luck. It was not without reason that the Olympic Games of Peking in 2008 started on the eighth day of the eighth month at eight minutes past eight.

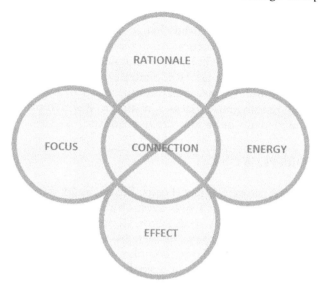

Figure 1.4   The Change Competence Model

Just as with the horizontal (reclining) 8, where vigilance plays a role, this also holds true for the vertical form.

In the vertical lemniscate, the upper loop frames the reason for the change (the Rationale) and the lower loop the results to be attained (the Effect). The lemniscate form clearly shows that the two cannot be seen independent from each other. The upper and lower loops meet in the Connection, the place where the literal and figurative conversion must be made through the change process.

The Horizontal Lemniscate—The Reclining Eight

The reclining 8 can be seen as the (mathematical) symbol for infinity. Without a beginning or an end, one situation flows into another. A recognizable aspect of reality: change as tripartite as seen by Lewin[10] is literally outdated. Organizational changes happen in increasingly more rapid succession, and often one change is the pre-stage or 'stepping stone' of the other. As a result, the intervals between changes become shorter and there is almost never a real break anymore. Many researchers therefore advocate to abandon the notion that change has a beginning and an end: the end is the beginning of the new.

Gastmans[11] sees the reclining form in Celtic knot motifs, among others. The inextricable or endless knot stands for continuity and perpetuity. Changes are not forever, but change is. The Buddhist infinity knot stands as a sign of a long life with a never-ending vigilance. In the Change Competence Model, this vigilance is seen in the continual review of what the organization is able to handle in terms of change capacity versus the requirements coming from the change vision.

The Connection, where the vertical and horizontal lemniscate meet, is seen as the heart, the heart of the change with the four other factors as its bloodstreams. If an obstruction occurs somewhere, this will lead to a reduced functioning of the whole. For example, a lack of consensus about the motivations for the change (Rationale) can never lead to the correct Focus. After all, should, for instance, the appearance of a new competitor be counteracted by redesigning processes leading to lowered prices, or should the attack be made with more innovative products?

FIVE FACTORS PLUS ONE

The five factors (Rationale, Effect, Focus, Energy and Connection) together describe an answer to Bower's two questions: *what it should be* and *how it should be accomplished*. A sixth factor, Context, can be added to this to clarify that changes must always be seen from the perspective of the relevant context. Change in a large, complex organization demands different things in many respects than in a small, transparent organization. The public domain places different requirements than does the business sector. A positive change history and much knowledge and experience with change provide a different starting point than a negative one and when change skills are lacking. Change stemming from a healthy ambition has different requirements than change by dire necessity. The Context factor stands for the 'starting value' and change's point of departure. The Context determines if a change is called for, and if so, to what degree. Therefore, the Context dictates the requirements of the change vision and the change capacity.

The Change Competence Model is framed by the sixth factor:

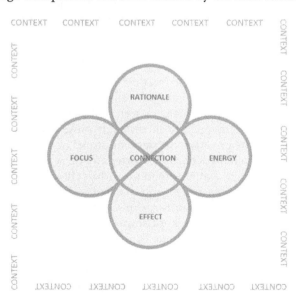

Figure 1.5   Change Competence within the relevant context

From the point of view of purposive change, Bower argues for a map for practitioners—a map for change. To answer his call, the Change Competence Model can be completed (made concrete) with the determining factors from the PROMIIC study.[12] It thus adds color and tone to the five factors or petals of the model. Thus, the model looks as follows:

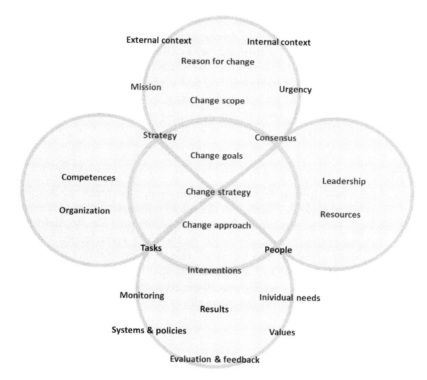

Figure 1.6   The five factors put into operation with PROMIIC

THE LEADING FACTORS PUT INTO OPERATION

Rationale

The internal and external context of the organization determines the reason for the change. Being able to clearly outline that reason demands knowledge of the external environment, the company's history, its development over the years and associated experiences, feelings, habits, routines and memories (the internal context). Once the context is outlined and the reason clear, the consequences for the mission can be determined. This analysis creates a sense of urgency: is it necessary to change (for example, to avoid bankruptcy) or does the change stem from a (new) ambition? After this, the scope of the change can be determined: the desired or necessary breadth and depth of the change.

Focus

Focus helps to convert the 'why' of the change to the 'what'; from change reason to change direction by means of strategy and the resulting structure, systems, operating processes, (prioritized) organizational values and goals, and also by exemplary behavior. In this way the strategy must provide clarity about which organizational or core competencies are to be utilized, given the necessity or ambition to change. The design of the organization, through the use of structures, systems and operational processes, must support the realization of the change by forming behavioral frameworks in line with the advocated change and change goals. The same process takes place at the individual and group level by describing tasks (and the associated responsibilities and authorities) in an appropriate way. Structures and systems can help bring about desired behavior and also play a role in perpetuating that behavior.

Energy

Consensus is a determining factor in the relationship between the Rationale and the Energy. If there is a sufficient degree of consensus, energy is created for the change. Inspiration, commitment and effort provide the fuel for the change. Leadership and resources, such as the right knowledge, skills and budget, will then make the change attainable. The people factor expresses the importance of the will and ability to change. If preparedness (the will) and readiness (the ability) are lacking, then no energy will be created or the energy will be quickly lost. In this case, the step from Energy to Effect cannot be taken.

Effect

The tasks, the work that must be done and the degree to which individuals are willing and able to contribute, also determine the shape and contents of the interventions or actions. These represent the concrete activities focused on changing the individual and the collective behavior for the benefit of the change. They determine the effect of the change, expressed by concrete results, but also determine emotions, perceptions and opinions. Monitoring, systems and policies play a significant role in the direction and perpetuation of changes. When interventions are used to achieve a certain result, the intermediate results (hard) must be monitored well, but monitoring must also and especially provide information about the (unforeseen) needs employees have (developed) during the implementation (soft results), in order to subsequently address these needs. Once the implementation phase has been completed, the change must be secured in the organization through systems and policies that stimulate the good behavior and extinguish the undesired behavior or at least diminish it. The way in which this is done must be in tune with the values and convictions of the employees. Evaluation and feedback show the effect of the change, both the desired as well as the undesired consequences. This can lead to an adjustment of the change goals or the adjustment of the rate of change. But they can also lead to an increase in the change capacity, for example, by developing individuals, increasing the budget (Energy) or prioritizing activities and organizational values (Focus).

Connection

The Connection forms the (beating) heart of the change. This is the connection between desirability and feasibility, the change vision and the change capacity. It's also the connection between goals and means, dreams and actions, facts and feelings. Integration and cohesion, translation and understanding form the core. Connection as a control function is shaped by the change goals, the change strategy and the change approaches. The Connection thus not only represents the heart, but also the traffic control tower of the change. In a symbolic sense, not a mathematical reality, the five factors (or petals) can be represented as a formula:

$$Change\ Competence = (Rationale \times Effect \times Focus \times Energy)^{Connection}$$

If the value of even one of the petals is zero or negative, there will be insufficient competence to change.

PREVIEW

Efficient or effective change depends on change competence. Rationale, Effect, Focus, Energy and Connection in conjunction with Context aid in understanding, handling and allowing the change process to work. The often-experienced gap between plan and execution can be bridged through the cohesion of these six factors. Terms such as robust, energetic, vital, active, flourishing and healthy are part of change competence. This vitality or health increases through the guiding and underlying success factors or 'levers' and decreases through failure factors or 'leaks.' When developing and harnessing change competence, the success factors must be developed and used as levers. But it is equally important to counter the failure factors and their influence. If all goes well, the bridge between plan and execution is built in a professional way.

Chapter 2 describes the failure and success factors, insights and phenomena related to Rationale, Effect, Focus, Energy and Connection. It draws concepts such as Focus and Rationale more to the foreground, and further fleshes these concepts out. Chapter 3 discusses the dynamic in change processes. The dynamic of a change process is illustrated from the perspective of a newly appointed leader and the classic first '100 days.' Dysfunctions are a central topic in Chapter 4; these are an organization's major or minor 'disorders' that stand in the way of change or require change. Chapter 5 describes twelve 'soft' and 'hard' leadership roles in change. All of these are associated with one of the six factors of the Change Competence Model. Chapter 6 emphasizes change strategies and change approaches: with what and how can changes take shape and be realized? In Chapter 7 we present a change competence case; in Chapter 8, we show how the change process under Anne's leadership has gone this past year and what the resulting prospects are.

NOTES

1. De Geus, A. Op weg naar de democratische organisatie: Loyaliteit en 'human talent' in een wereld van downsizing, efficiency focus en reengineering. Interview with Arie de Geus (former head of Shell Strategic Planning Group). Acquired on April 18, 2013, via http://www.pearson-education.nl/winkler/pdf/Op_weg_naar_de_democratische_organisatie.pdf.
2. Beer, M., & Nohria, N. (2000). Cracking the code of change. *Harvard Business Review, 78 (3)*, 133–141.
3. Smith, M. E. (2002). Success rates for different types of organizational change. *Performance Improvement, 41 (1)*, 26–33.
4. Ten Have, W. D. (2000). *Strategie-implementatie in Nederland: De feiten.* Utrecht, NL: Berenschot.
5. Aspesi, C., & Vardhan, D. (1999). Brilliant strategy, but can you execute? *McKinsey Quarterly, 1*, 89–99.
6. Mankins, M. C., & Steele, R. (2005). Turning great strategy into great performance. *Harvard Business Review, 83 (7/8)*, 64–72.
7. Bower, J. L. (2000). The purpose of change: A commentary on Jensen and Senge. In M. Beer & N. Nohria (eds.), *Breaking the code of change* (pp. 83–95). Boston, MA: Harvard Business School Press.
8. Bower, J. L. (2000). The purpose of change: A commentary on Jensen and Senge. In M. Beer & N. Nohria (eds.), *Breaking the code of change* (pp. 83–95). Boston, MA: Harvard Business School Press.
9. Spanjersberg, M., Van den Hoek, A., Veldhuijzen van Zanten, E., & Van Wingerden, R. (2011). *Systeemdenken in de praktijk: De kunst van het verbinden.* Utrecht, NL: Stili Novi.
10. Lewin, K. (1951). *Field theory in social science: Selected theoretical papers.* D. Cartwright (ed.). New York, NY: Harper & Row.
11. Gastmans, F. (2001). Lemniscaat als symbool. Acquired on February 2, 2013, via http://www.lemniscaatacademie.be/Lemniscaatacademie/LEMNISCAAT_files/lemniscaat_als_symbool_4.1.pdf
12. Ten Have, S., Ten Have, W. D., & Janssen, B. (2009). *Het veranderboek: 70 vragen van managers over organisatieverandering.* Amsterdam, NL: Mediawerf.

2 Failure and Success Factors

The available change competence and thereby the quality of the five petals, individually and jointly, can make or break a successful organizational change. Within that competence to change, Rationale, Effect, Focus and Energy can be seen as the arteries of the change; the Connection—literally and figuratively—its heart. If the heart is not beating and pumping, nothing or next to nothing is done; there is no effective change. If the coronary arteries are not working, you have the same result. These problems can vary based on cause and kind. Solutions have a comparable variety. An organization can develop a blockage and have a 'heart attack' due to neglect, an unhealthy 'lifestyle' or the sudden onset of severe stress. Sometimes you can see it coming, and other times the process is insidious, like a 'silent killer.' Sometimes there is a warning or there can be an early and orderly intervention. This may or may not require a 'medical' procedure: sometimes losing weight and living a healthier lifestyle are enough; sometimes stenting and medication are necessary. In other cases, it is fatal or indirectly life threatening. In those cases, the reaction is more drastic and often more extensive: open heart surgery. The path to recovery is longer and often more fragile. Sometimes, there really is full recovery, and sometimes there is persistent dependence or damage.

Similar observations and notes can be seen with organizations and change. Health, effectiveness and success are the result of an adequate change competence; failure, ineffectiveness and breakdown are the result of a lack thereof. Often at the start of a change initiative, one or more (sub) factors have not been developed, or if so, inadequately. Leadership styles that do not (or inadequately) connect to the needs for change, rigid structures, unclear prioritization of the goals, illogical sequencing of the change and a rate of change that is too high, can each (partially) block an organization's change competence and thereby undermine its change success. These blockages can develop because the organization does not know how to detect the early signs of problems. This may be caused when feedback from the bottom rungs of the organization does not reach the top, but also because signals that *are* being heard are deliberately ignored or downplayed with platitudes such as 'it won't be so bad' or 'it will sort itself out.' The inability or lack of willingness to see potential areas needing attention may itself be the greatest blockage of all.

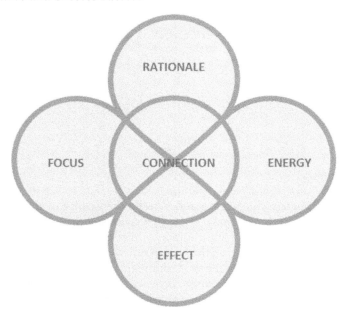

Figure 2.1   The Change Competence Model

It is extremely important for organizations to know what factors are in play. Sometimes there are so many, however, that they can't see the wood for the trees. Applying structure to the jungle of factors is therefore of the utmost importance for clearing these blockages. Below, based on the Change Competence Model, the different failure and success factors are highlighted per petal, in order to apply structure, logic and causality.

RATIONALE

The Rationale translates as the *reason* for movement, and stands for the idea behind a change, in a logical and visionary sense. It pertains to the cognitive and the affective, the rational and the emotional, the hard and the soft. The Rationale must provide the *reason for change* and be a *reason to change*. Cognitively, the reasoning, expressed in a business case, in strategic logic or in vision, must be correct. Affectively, it must be touching and appealing. Much can be done to achieve this, but there is also much that can stand in its way or impede it.

Failure Factors

The first failure factor in relation to the Rationale is future shock. The image or story of the outlined future and the associated change is so overwhelming that it is too much for the 'recipients.' Instead of inspiration, movement and enthusiasm, the recipients are paralyzed, run away or have a 'heart attack.' In other cases the Rationale is not established or is put in place without much thought. The first occurs when there is a paralysis by analysis. Too much information is gathered and compiled, which creates an information overload. And whereas the story still may be correct, the understanding and necessity for the change remain far out of reach. A perception of necessity is another failure factor here. If there is no perception of necessity—a sense of urgency—the organization will then not step into action as quickly.

Another obstacle stems from a bias for action. The organization rushes through the image and opinion formation phases; jumps to conclusions. It relies on previous experiences, in-house expertise and pattern recognition. It is then easier to miss the specific context.

Another failure factor with the Rationale is the non-event.[1] A change is announced with much fanfare, but followed by a deafening silence. Often, the change is associated with a (popular) management concept, such as the Balanced Scorecard (BSC), coaching or Lean. Sometimes such concepts fit and work, but too often they are an empty shell and usually do not answer the specific issues at play for the organization. The organization is mobilized with much noise and entertainment, but after a period of time the initiative peters out or is run alongside the 'real' work. If an organization has undergone a series of non-events, this often has a structurally demotivating effect. This comes back to bite it when real action finally has to be taken.

The tendency to opt for the quick hit, whether or not under pressure, is also a failure factor. In this case, managers want to quickly change the organization or culture. This happens without attention to a good diagnosis and the null hypothesis[2] that change is not necessary. The real motivation, insofar as there is one, stays out of the picture: superficiality prevails. Such change would be similar to a doctor that starts to stent arbitrarily without knowing exactly which arteries are blocked.

Sometimes a possible motivation for the change is nipped in the bud. Those in power find change to be threatening, disagreeable or risky. A witch-hunt ensues. The change-seeking individuals are relativized, disqualified and marginalized: "that cannot be substantiated," "he always has something to complain about," "that's not loyal," or "she just has an axe to grind."

Another, comparable, failure factor is the biased evaluation: the rapid acceptance of proof that supports one's own or existing position and suppositions and the disproportionate negative evaluation of proof to the contrary. An extension of this is selective memory: the creation of a new Rationale by using specific parts of previous changes (that by itself were successful) as the basis for change; one, however, that is hampered by low motivation for change as a result of past failures and diverging interests that one tends to avoid. So everyone sits on the fence.

Another failure factor is simply the lack of a vision and strategy. The absence of a guiding framework within which the question of, if there must be change, and if so what, is answered. There is an inability to form a vision of the future and there is fixation on the here and now. Sometimes the formulation of a Rationale for the change is "prevented" by organizational silence. Informational flows are limited and inhibited; no one speaks his mind and there is a lack of overview and insight.

False consensus is a frequently occurring failure factor at the Rationale level. Not infrequently do leaders overestimate the degree to which others, their followers, share and endorse their vision, convictions and choices. Another failure factor is meaninglessness. The Rationale is then filled (up) with values and expressions that no one is or could be against, such as "there must be more flexibility," "there must be greater efficiency," "more innovation," and "more customer-orientation." These do not give a specific direction to the organization in question and do not create sustainable movement.

Yet another failure factor is the lack of commitment to the change the organization has experienced by top management or the board of directors. The lack of commitment often stems from dynamic conservatism.[3] Those currently in authority react to the changes by focusing on protecting and maintaining the status quo.[4] Aside from inactive leadership, unidentified traumas are a failure factor because they can erode the current Rationale's raison d'être at a cognitive level and undermine readiness for change at the affective level.

In line with this are such failure factors as: *stare decisis* (Latin: stand by that which has been previously decided), self-interest, chauvinistic conditioning and Machiavelli's change has no constituency. Stare decisis refers to law and pertains to the precedent set by previous decisions, about their "binding" effect for judges, who subsequently have to pass a judgment. Translated to change, it means that new changes, when seen in relation to previous changes, are viewed as obvious or comparable, i.e., terms of use and necessity. But a Rationale is not necessarily transferable. Every change initiative needs its *own* reason and motivation, given the particular situation and characteristics. In this context, reference can also be made to the aforementioned null hypothesis[5] of Van Witteloostuijn: those who support the change or wish to initiate the change must provide specific proof to demonstrate the necessity, desirability and attainability of the change. In other words: the change is really only implemented if there is a thought-out and plausible, if not convincing, change case. The conservative Lord Falkland made a well-chosen statement in this respect in 1641: *"When it is not necessary to change, it is necessary not to change."*

Self-interest refers to the position that change can be good for others or even for the entire system, but will not be welcomed unless it is demonstrably to our own benefit. This can occur on an individual level, but it can also stand in the way of an effective Rationale. Top management plays for time, while the organization has all the reason it needs to get moving. Recent examples can be found in the worlds of housing cooperatives, health care and of the banking sector.

Chauvinistic conditioning takes the position that 'how we do things is the right way.' If you are one of us, and you support or initiate change, then you are loyal. Machiavelli's statement expresses that the interest of a small minority in retaining their own position of power within the current situation, is often much stronger than the interest of the majority to give a leg up to an uncertain alternative.

Some failure factors can also be compared with cholesterol[6]—certainly in a model that can be seen as a pumping heart (Connection) and a collection of arteries (the other four petals), where a healthy blood flow is determinant for proper functioning. Just like a high a cholesterol level, the failure factors can be seen as silent killers. Cholesterol causes the arteries to become clogged with virtually no real external symptoms for a long period of time. Examples respective to the Rationale-relevant silent killers are an unclear strategy, conflicting priorities and the lack of a clear and inspiring direction and dialogue.

In connection with this we refer to the failure factor that is called threats to coherent action.[7] In that case, the formulated Rationale does not take a hold because the cognitive and emotional processing within the organization is missing. This happens to managers with a strong command style and a top-down approach, i.e., managers who are directive. The rational and symbolic aspects that ensure the image and feeling of co-production and ownership are missing from the process within which the Rationale and the associated vision and strategy are developed.

The following are the success factors associated with the Rationale. As with the other four (Effect, Focus, Energy and Connection), this frequently pertains to 'independent' success factors and sometimes to factors that are the direct reverse or inverse of the failure factors described. Take stare decisis as an example: by reversing the burden of proof and imposing this, instead, as per Van Witteloostuijn and 'his' null hypothesis, onto those proposing a change, it is then interpreted as a success factor.

Success Factors

A success factor associated with the Rationale is the ability to formulate a guiding vision. Such a vision must be clear and appealing and provide guidance within the organization itself *and* ensure trust and respect for the stakeholders. An actual guiding vision can fulfill the strategic, tactical and ethical functions of guide, reminder and conscience in the thoughts and deeds of the organization. A guiding vision must meet five[8] conditions:

- Coherence founded on reality;
- Credibility and challenge;
- Stakeholder satisfaction;
- Leadership involvement;
- Public visibility.

People often struggle to understand the difference between vision, mission and strategy. The *vision* describes how the organization sees the world: What is the relevant context for the organization and its future? What are the developments to be anticipated in the future? The *mission* stands for the function the organization wishes to fill in that world: What is the raison d'être that the company possesses or strives for in the world? What is its desired contribution? The *strategy* describes the path along which the organization wishes to realize that function, role and position. The vision pertains to the context and the mission to the higher purpose within that context. Together they answer the *why* and the *what* questions. Strategy pertains to the realization of the higher purpose through setting priorities and the concrete goals associated with those priorities. The Rationale stands for the change reason, and thus contains the vision and the mission—the higher purpose.

A good mission is clear as well as appealing. The cognitive and the affective, the rational and the emotional are well provided for. In reality, many missions (and strategies) do not do what they are intended to do: *"They imply a sense of direction, clarity of thinking, and unity that rarely exists."*[9] What is often missing in particular is a sense of mission and a goal that is clear and valuable. The former calls for a mission that reflects the organizational values and the personal values and motives. The latter revolves around an appealing mission that must be clear, ambitious, challenging and goal-oriented.

Collins and Porras[10] list four ways to create such missions:

- Targeting;
- Common enemy;
- Role model;
- Internal transformation.

Targeting refers to the definition of a clear and concrete goal and working toward the realization of that goal. Examples are the ambition of the supermarket chain Walmart to double its own profits to a billion dollars within four years at the end of the seventies, and the objective of the Dutch National Soccer team to become European Champion in 2008. These missions generally have a limited shelf life. If the target is achieved or if it takes too long to achieve, there needs to be a reformulation of the mission to prevent the energy from ebbing away.

In the second way, the energy is generated by working together to beat a *common enemy*. In this way, Philips sets itself up against the Japanese competitor Sony in a number of change processes, Pepsi cultivates the image of Coca-Cola as a rival, and a number of years ago the supermarket chain Laurus made beating Ahold its goal. This approach works particularly well for organizations that want to become the number one. A major disadvantage however can be that such a destructive approach of "being at war" can also invoke negative feelings in the employees and in the long-run is not very inspiring.

Role model missions are often focused on excellent examples from other sectors. For example, an organization wants to become the "Mercedes" among business real estate brokers. For these missions, the issue is to select appealing models, or better yet, examples that are obvious to everyone. The risk is that the role model chosen may lose its reputation due to incidents or scandals. As was the case with Enron, which prior to the fall was frequently named by reputable writers and consulting firms as the example of an excellent organization and was embraced as such by other organizations.

Finally, there are the missions of *internal transformation*, which are particularly effective in older organizations that have to drastically change themselves in order to become (or stay) competitive and healthy. Often there is a clear need that makes an internal transformation crucial—for example, in the publishing world, where missions have been drastically changed to be able to lead the transformation from a traditional publisher to a multimedia business.

An adequate Rationale also demands that the organization breaks with the present. Frame-breaking questions, cognitive diversity and techniques such as futuring, visioning and storytelling[11] contribute to this. The first two are part of the strategic thinking process needed to identify and define change.[12] This pertains to the creative, diverging and synthesizing processes versus the analytic, converging and conventional processes of strategic planning. Futuring is a systematic thought process about the future and objective world, to include expectations, possibilities and threats in a shared and fruitful reference framework. Visioning, on the other hand, works from the inside out; it is a stretching exercise. The question is what must be changed in the current situation in order to have raison d'être in the future and to realize growth and progress. Storytelling is the translation of the message about motives, change and goals into an appealing, challenging story that touches people and stays with them.

The determining factors of such techniques are also visible in the dimensions of transformational leadership.[13] This type of leadership transforms individuals and groups of employees to make them more receptive to change and to increase their capacity to deal with change. The dimensions referred to, or success factors, are:

- Articulating a vision;
- Fostering group goals;
- High performance expectations;
- Intellectual stimulation.

The Rationale is also concerned with the legitimacy of the change. Is the why tenable, acceptable and appealing? Here the symbolic role of the leader plays a significant role: an attention focusing process must always be provided. This can be done by making the necessity for change visible through worsened achievements and financial results or significantly changed market conditions. Information building, such as through market research or policy analysis, can be an effective tool.

Heifetz and Laurie[14] list five success factors from the leadership perspective that are relevant to the Rationale:

- Identify the adaptive challenge and frame key questions and issues;
- Let the organization feel external pressures within a range it can stand;
- Challenge current roles and prevent new roles to be filled in too quickly;
- Expose conflict and let it emerge;
- Challenge unproductive norms and values.

Important tactics and success factors at the level of the Rationale are also rational persuasion and legitimating tactics. The first deals with the use of logical arguments and actual proof to support the Rationale—think of the formulation of a strategic logic and the development of business models. In legitimating tactics, the organization's own authority or the policy, its current practices and traditions, are used to support the Rationale.

EFFECT

Effect stands for the intended or experienced (concrete) effects on the various stakeholders, both in the short and long term. This involves advantages and disadvantages, positive and negative results, perceptions and feelings on an individual level and within their relevant, social and organizational environment.

Failure Factors

On the effect level, the personal situation, perspectives and perceptions of individuals and groups that will have to deal with the change are significant determining factors in the valuing of the change. An initial failure factor is that change goals are too abstract or disconnected for those who have to actually deal with the change in practice.[15] Sometimes this is due to a lack of clarity at the practical level, and sometimes because it is overly operationalized.[16] In the latter case, this often has to do with the (large) quantity of performance indicators used to attempt to make the change concrete. But it is mainly about the quality and acceptance of those indicators. To be able to understand and accept the effect of a change, there must be an interactive process in which these indicators are connected to the mission, the strategy and the change goals. The employees must experience what it means to them in real terms and that the challenge and reality are balanced. They need be able to see their own contribution to the bigger picture and understand what to do with it in their day-to-day work.

Another failure factor is that the change could infringe the psychological contract, whether in fact or in the perception of the stakeholders.[17] In that case, the change causes the (perceived) obligations to not be fulfilled. This pain is often in not being involved or consulted. Instead of an open discussion and possible renewal of the contract, managers in some cases choose to mask the consequences and magnify the Rationale compared to the Effect.

The quality of the psychological contract depends on the employees' degree and form of the commitment. Among these, various forms[18] are to be distinguished:

- Affective commitment: refers to the emotional connection of employees, their identification and involvement with the organization. Employees with a strong affective commitment continue to work for an organization because they want to.
- Continuance commitment: refers to an understanding of the costs associated with leaving the organization. Employees with a high continuance commitment stay with an organization because they have to.
- Normative commitment: refers to a feeling of obligation to continue being employed. Employees with a high normative commitment feel that they are expected to remain with the organization.

One should be aware of the effect that the change may have on the degree and form of the commitment. It may be a conscious choice to exchange affective commitment for continuance commitment through a difficult intervention. But that choice can also be very harmful. In shaping the change and the accompanying process, it is important to provide psychological contracts and to have the appropriate and necessary commitment for a successful change process.

Another failure factor is a lack of change-related self-efficacy.[19] This form of self-efficacy represents the degree to which one is convinced of one's own capacity to be able to adequately and efficiently deal with a change situation. Lacking change-related self-efficacy has a negative impact on the openness, direction and acceptance of changes.

The feeling of having control over one's own environment using one's own actions and conduct is referred to as action control and is also a failure factor within the Effect. When an individual feels connected to a goal, decision, change or strategy and there is action control, the individual will generally develop an action orientation. On the other hand, if an individual does not feel connected to the goal, decision or strategy, a state orientation usually sets in.[20] In an action orientation, one is focused on factors that help realize the goal, decision or strategy (e.g., developing a way or approach to achieve the goal, blocking emotions that impede focused action and being open for information relevant to achieving the goal). With a state orientation, the focus stays on factors that do not contribute to achieving the goal; the individual sticks to counterproductive emotions, frames of reference and information.

The status quo bias, selective memory, confirmation bias and biased evaluation can also create an impediment at the Effect level. Status quo bias stands for the people's tendency to be more afraid of potential loss than to becoming enthusiastic about the prospect of attractive progress or profit. Selective memory leads to particularly remembering facts and experiences that confirm one's own beliefs and position. Confirmation bias stands for the tendency to look for opinions and facts that confirm one's own vision, convictions and experiences. Biased evaluation involves the quick and preferential acceptance of evidence that supports one's personal or current position and assumptions, combined with ignoring any evidence to the contrary.

At the effect level, the motivation for change is also hampered by the failure factors of: immediate change costs, cannibalization costs and the comfort of cross-subsidization.[21] With immediate costs, for example, one does see the long-term career possibilities; however, having to act in the short term is a taller order. Cannibalization costs refer to the phenomenon that the change does provide something that benefits one interest (view, goal, person or group), but that it also does so at the expense of another interest. Comfort of cross-subsidization can come to play when a problem business (unit) is being subsidized by rents from another successful part of the business. This does not create a real motivation for change (especially since what you have is a known, and what you might get, an unknown).

Other failure factors at the level of Effect have been exposed when studying cultural change.[22] The first is the hijacked process: the organization-wide process of change is sometimes hijacked by managers or organizational units. Under the guise of the broader change, personal or other objectives deviating from the original goal, such as cost reduction or restructuring, are pursued instead.

Yet another failure factor is the lack of attention to symbolism. In a technical sense, a change program is based on the right goals and principles, but runs aground because it goes counter to more unconscious, deeper images, feelings and values. If an "outside" manager starts up a professionalization program in a family business, this can also be experienced as disqualification of the family members that have led the business for generations.

Some failure factors at the Effect level are associated with coping mechanisms. Coping mechanisms that are active, but counter to the change, are sabotage and exit. In sabotage, for example, a change program is made to look ridiculous or everything that goes wrong in the organization is blamed on that program. Exit means that people leave the organization in reaction to the change—often literally and physically, sometimes 'only' mentally. Often these are good individuals who are vital for the change, who can easily find work elsewhere. This is a failure factor squared: by its symbolic impact and the actual loss.

'BOHICA' and paralysis are passive and negative coping mechanisms. BOHICA stands for Bend Over, Here It Comes Again. People wait for the change to blow over. This is not always a negative reaction in all respects. It often also leads to people focusing on their 'normal work.' The second reaction is often more harmful. Paralysis leads to people not contributing to the change and no longer being able to perform their normal work and routine activities well.

Success Factors

Success factors at the Effect level have to do with the concept of workplace recovery. This concept is focused on having the transition run smoothly at the organizational level and the adjustment at an individual level. In a change process, each organization and each individual simultaneously experiences forces aimed at maintaining the status quo and forces aimed at change.[23] These forces act in opposite directions, and during a change process, the balance shifts from one moment to the next. Therefore, workplace recovery is aimed at two tasks:

- Weakening or reducing the forces that maintain the old;
- Strengthening or promoting the forces that help develop the new.

The adjustment to a transition doesn't happen in an instant, and generally has a 'fading in and out' character. In the beginning, the forces aimed at maintaining the status quo are generally dominant. This can be seen in forms of resistance and passivity, the lack of will to act. Over time, the innovative forces become stronger and help in letting go of the old and moving toward the new.

In a transition, both forces aim at both the emotional as well as the business dimensions of the change. The emotional aspects (emotional realities) pertain to how people experience the change. Good leaders make sure they observe the emotions associated with a transition and understand how they influence functioning. The business aspects (business imperatives) pertain to what must be done to realize the organizational goals, and thereby achieve success. This includes, for example, setting concrete goals, supporting reward systems and work processes and communication patterns.

When the two tasks (the weakening and strengthening of forces) and the two dimensions (the emotional and the business) are combined, four success factors are created: empathy, engagement, energy and enforcement (see Table 2.1).[24]

Table 2.1   The four elements of workplace recovery (Marks, 2006)

		Tasks	
		Weakening the old	Strengthening the new
Levels	Emotional Realities	Empathy	Energy
	Business Imperatives	Engagement	Enforcement

- Empathy means that management understands that change is difficult, and appreciates the difficulties that employees may experience in letting go of their old certainties and routines. This begins to take shape by identifying and sharing individual problems in the process of adjustment and transition for example. Other ways are offering workshops and coaching aimed at increasing awareness around certain problems and emotional difficulties. Thought can furthermore be given to using symbols, ceremonies and forums in which the termination of the old is the central theme.
- Engagement stands for the development of understanding and support when saying goodbye to the old and accepting the new reality. This can be done, for example, through communication and by offering opportunities to truly participate in the transition. Another way is diagnosing and eliminating things that hamper individual adaptation, such as fear of reduction of the terms of employment and of development possibilities.
- Energy is the inspiration and involvement of people to let them contribute to the realization of the new reality and the accompanying ambitions and possibilities. A first way is by defining and clarifying the new vision with a different and better organization at its heart. In addition, it can be shaped by creating learning opportunities and achieving success in the short-term, both of which make the advantages of the new reality visible.
- Enforcement refers to confirming and enhancing perceptions, expectations and behavior appropriate to the new organization. This can be done, for example, by involving people in the translation of the vision into concrete improvements in their work and working conditions. Another way is to bring systems and processes in line with the new reality of the organization.

By paying attention to these four success factors, leaders can ensure that the desired effect is created for individuals and specific groups. This makes it possible to achieve the necessary adjustment at the individual and group level for the successful transition of an organization. The combined attention helps letting go and accepting, understanding and adjusting.

Another success factor in bringing about the right Effect with change is yield, which stands for the visible or to be experienced results, rewards or benefits that are, or can be, associated with the change. Being able to make the change concrete is an important success factor for leaders.[25] For many changes, the necessity and the ambition behind them are muffled. They remain abstract or at best restricted to a concept at the Rationale level. By making the necessity or ambition concrete, people are enabled to formulate their own contributing intentions and actions.

From Effect, important tactics for influencing people with the importance of the change are: inspirational appeals, exchange, personal appeals and pressure.[26]

Inspirational appeals generate enthusiasm by connecting with or appealing to the values, ideals or ambitions of individuals or groups. This is particularly transformational. Exchange is more transactional, and is focused on the granting or holding out the prospect of favors or other positive compensations in return for supporting the change. Personal appeals rely on the personal relationship, loyalty or friendship. Pressure stands for the use of demands, threats or frequent reminders to get someone to cooperate in the change.

Research[27] shows that clarity and a good operationalization (from Rationale to Effect) is an important necessary condition. But an operationalized change goal probably works especially well when the goal is relatively remote from the current situation. In that case, it is challenging and demanding, and will more quickly get the necessary attention and priority.

Another key success factor is reviewing the (intermediate) outcomes of a change process from angles. This means that those outcomes must be weighed and guided not only in terms of achievement, but also in terms of performance and acceptance. Realization refers to the degree to which the intentional change has been completed according to plan; achievement refers to the degree to which that change has achieved the intended effects. Acceptance refers to the degree to which that which has been realized is satisfactory to stakeholders and interested parties.

Kotter[28] posits different success factor associated with the Effect of the change. The first is to generate short-term successes. Generating sufficient successes quickly enough to (further) reduce cynicism, pessimism and skepticism, be unambiguous and appeal to people on issues that really affect them. The second factor is consolidating improvements, thereby creating a basis for more change (if necessary) by helping people create change wave after change wave, until the vision has become a reality. Or by not allowing the sense of urgency to evaporate through difficult parts of the transformation—the larger emotional barriers in particular—by not avoiding them. Those in charge of the change strategy must also prevent premature exhaustion from setting in by eliminating unnecessary work. The third success factor is anchoring new approaches in the culture. This means ensuring that people continue to act according to the new standards and values, despite the understandable appeal of tradition (and previous experiences and routines). This can be done for example by socializing new colleagues, establishing goal-oriented rewards, promoting employees and influencing employees emotionally.

FOCUS

Focus refers to the *direction* of movement: the frameworks and coordinates that concretely indicate what is expected in terms of behavior, organization and cooperation. The direction of movement is manifested in, for example, the strategy, structure and organizational values. The translation into tasks makes the required skill level concrete at an individual and group level. Focus comes into being in and by exemplary behavior, upheld principles, setting of priorities and the applicable selection criteria and by dealing with conflicts of interest.

Failure Factors

An initial failure factor lies in uncontrolled and uncoordinated efforts. People who work locally with an apparently clear objective or intervention are bombarded with conflicting, contradictory assignments and questions. These often originate from different departments or portfolio holders.[29] The conflicting priorities (related to the goals pursued) may also constitute a failure factor. This also results in priority proliferation (everything is important).

In addition, not only goals or efforts, but also (organizational) values can conflict or be inadequately prioritized. This not only leads to a shaky basis for decisions and resource allocation but also to confusion and inefficiency, because it is not clear which activities and behaviors have priority over others.

Other failure factors[30] associated with Focus are poor vertical communication, inadequate down-the-line leadership and a lack of coordination across functions, divisions, boundaries and interfaces. In a change situation, the last mentioned point may pertain to the existing organization, the change program or the relationship between the two, and thus involves the structural or organizational hygiene.[31]

An important failure factor also lies in creating the wrong kind of Focus: ritualization of the change.[32] This ritualization can be created from the assumption that a radical change of the organization generally demands the necessary time and attention. Therefore, organizations plan their interventions over a longer period of time, for example, a number of activities per quarter. As a result, it is often transformed into a ritual; it is not thought through and interventions do not take place depending on the need and insight of the specific moment. Schaffer and Thomson[33] posit that an important reason for failure lies in the fact that activity-oriented change programs are generally used more often than result-oriented change programs. They maintain that working with an activity orientation confuses results with resources and processes with outcomes.

Another failure factor, also due to a mistaken Focus, is change originating in an ivory tower. Top management designs the change, where the translation to the elements in the Focus petal takes place without insight into the reality that people have to deal with elsewhere in the organization. The elaborated approach does not do justice to possibilities and limitations in the field and is often shortly after launch already labeled unfeasible and unrealistic.

The existing Focus can also be a failure factor. Strebel[34] identifies four factors wherein this can work against the change:

- Rigid structures and systems that are expressed in organizational forms, technologies and resources that are actually not designed for change.

- Narrow-minded ways of thinking that are expressed in values, behaviors and skills that are not open to change.
- Entrenched (sub)cultures that cannot be adjusted or reviewed in response to an emerging change.
- Counterproductive changes influenced by precedents from the organizational history or other, often illegitimate, motives that in any case have nothing to do with the change itself and the need associated with that change.

These factors contribute to a syndrome (collection of failure factors) that can be described as the tail wagging the dog.[35] This is the case when the guiding convictions and values do not drive the strategy and actions, but actually are driven by the existing convictions. Here, the dog does not wag his tail; the tail wags the dog. This can be prevented by making the guiding convictions particularly audible, visible and tangible in the manners, rules and procedures, behavior management, rewards, appreciation and systems. The more clearly and convincingly this happens, the less room there is for determining the long-term prospect of the organization by the rules for daily survival.

Yet another failure factor is behavioral misalignment. This often occurs because those taking the initiative for a (cultural) change clearly state what the intention is, set the frameworks, but do not act accordingly themselves. The trustworthiness and sincerity of the leaders are then quickly put into doubt. To prevent this, it is important that those taking the initiative not only ask themselves what they want or what is needed, but also what they are able and willing to achieve. After that, they must demonstrate by word and deed that they are determined to bridge the gap between the desired and current situation.

Related to this is the failure factor of lip service, which refers to the phenomenon that the core concepts or guiding (organizational) values are heard, but not internalized.[36] They talk the talk, but don't walk the walk. For example, the organization talks a lot about being client-oriented, but this does not mean anything to the employees, and they also do not act any more client-oriented than before. This can be avoided by letting people participate in the process in which the concepts or values are shaped. If these are connected to real-life situations, personal concerns, problems or dilemmas, then they are lent content as well as shape. This way they come to life and while working, become part of the personal mental baggage. If there is already a lip service issue, then it is important to ask people about what their slogans and values mean in terms of their own actions and functioning.

Another failure factor connected with Focus is the one-sided devotion to hard wiring for creating new frameworks. Hard wiring[37] is the designing of a new organization with a formal set of structures, systems, processes and policies. Such a one-sided orientation ignores the social and behavioral components that are (also) involved in the change. Hard wiring by itself is not sufficient for the creation of the cognitive reorientation needed for a change process. The alternative is culturally sensitive design. This means that cultural framing and soft structuring must be provided prior to the hard wiring. Cultural framing is the diagnosing of the organization's hidden problems and challenges. Soft structuring stands for the preparation of the organization by developing the necessary changeability (Effect) and creating or restoring the social foundation in order to give the new structure a solid foundation. Hard wiring must be followed by retrospecting, which stands for the frequent evaluation and interpretation of the structure and culture as the basis for adjusting, embedding, learning and improving.

Sometimes, too much (individual) thinking stands in the way of working (together). Dysfunctional smartness[38] can undermine the common behavioral framework. The direction of movement is then repeatedly questioned. An excess of critical thinking and stubbornness can impede vigorous collective action. As a counterpart, functional stupidity is welcome with an eye toward coherence, direction and efficiency. The sixty-four thousand dollar question is where one begins and the other ends. Goffee and Jones[39] warn that even the Focus of Google (just like that of other clever collectives) in the form of their successful philosophy can deteriorate into a rigid doctrine or ideology that is resistant to new ideas and ways of looking at the world. This is also referred to as chauvinistic conditioning. This is the dark side of strong cultures, which has recently also confronted organizations such as UBS, Barclays and Olympus.[40]

Success Factors

An overarching success factor for Focus is that of prevailing circumstances or strong situational cues.[41] The determining conditions in the organization must suit the proposed change. If entrepreneurship is to be enhanced, then values, structures and reward mechanism must contribute to this individually and collectively. The same applies to model behavior. Leaders and other key players have an important role in the transfer of behavioral frameworks and the direction of movement. What they do and do not do has a strong symbolic and practical meaning for others within the 'system.' If they are aware of this role and its meaning, they can live the desired behavior, provide the right example. This way, others become socialized and a cognitive reorientation through modeling can take place.

A tool for providing the necessary Focus and Connection is a Transition Management Team (TMT).[42] A TMT must ensure congruency in actions, operations and emotions inherent to the change. Often, a TMT in particular provides boxes of containment that are necessary with change to provide for the desired clarity, space, safety and freedom. With this, a number of important success factors[43] form the simple rules:

- How-to rules: rules that describe which behavior and which operating processes create the distinctiveness of the organization.

- Boundary rules: rules that ensure that people focus on the right opportunities in the market as well as describe what falls outside the scope.
- Priority rules: rules that help managers and employees prioritize when making choices between options or requirements.
- Timing rules: rules that ensure that people and units within the organization are in step with each other, acting jointly.
- Exit rules: rules that help in making decisions about terminating activities or ceasing to pursue certain goals.

If such rules are missing, the execution and realization of the change becomes less likely. Research into the (failure of) strategy-implementation illustrates this.[44] It shows, for example, that unclear accountabilities for the execution, organizational silos and culture block good execution. In addition, Neilson and Pasternack[45] see Focus (in combination with Effect) as determinant for a successful implementation. Based on their studies, they suggest four building blocks:

- Decision rights: creating clarity when dealing with decision-making authority;
- Information: designing informational flows;
- Motivators: aligning motivators;
- Structure: adjusting the structure.

Among the characteristics of such organizations they suggest that everyone in the organization should have a clear idea of the decisions and actions that he or she is responsible for and that information flows freely through the organization; internal organizational boundaries must not be an obstacle.

ENERGY

Energy is the ability of the organization to change and provides the fuel for the change. It is the synthesis between the preparedness (willingness) and readiness (ability) of employees, which under the influence of leadership and availability of resources partly determine the feasibility of the change. This can involve 'hard' organizational elements such as physical resources and budget, but also 'softer,' more psychological elements such as readiness for change and trust.

The degree of consensus and leadership also determine the Energy: Is it possible to stand together for the same thing and to bring people together under the same umbrella? If this fails, Energy is sapped off, it will work counterproductively or an impasse or infighting results. In addition the importance of adequate resources in terms of budget, means, knowledge and experience should not be underestimated. Research by Mankins and Steele,[46] among others, places these factors in the top five when it comes to non-realization of goals.

Failure Factors

Two key failure factors[47] with Energy are product without process and process without product. Process without product occurs when the organization immerses itself in discussions, analyses and exploration without arriving at substantive insights about the culture and what is being pursued—let alone taking any action. This can be avoided by ensuring fewer words and more actions. Product without process is characterized for example by a cultural change achieved by a strong focus on the production of physical products such as posters, notecards, intranet pages and booklets with the new culture. Writing up the information is not the same as transferring it, embedding it, living through it and internalizing it—let alone acting based on it. These issues are about means: if there is product without process, the means become the goal. To avoid this, new convictions and values must be experienced. They must be given meaning by linking them to problems and solutions that are truly meaningful to employees in the respective context or work environment.

Another factor that can have a negative influence on Energy in a change process is treating the symptoms[48] or 'shifting the burden.' A deeper problem causes symptoms that need attention themselves. The problem itself is difficult to identify and address (lack of clarity, high costs). The burden of making a good diagnosis is shifted aside; easier and less expensive solutions are sought. Those solutions alleviate the symptoms, but exacerbate the underlying problem, also because management focuses attention on those symptoms. The system loses energy and motivation, the wrong problem is being addressed. Examples include automation (of a problem), cost reduction or structure modification. The recommendation to management: beware of treating the symptoms.

Other failure factors[49] are identified by research on functional and dysfunctional cultures. Energy does not flourish in cultures that are approving, conventional or dependent. Such cultures block or frustrate energy and the associated creativity, innovation, experiments and personal initiatives. In an approval culture, conflicts are avoided and (at a superficial level) everyone is particularly kind. Members have the feeling that they must agree with others or that their behavior and decisions must be approved by others. In a conventional culture, conservatism, tradition and bureaucratic control are what it is all about. Members must adapt to the prevailing order, they must follow the rules and leave a 'good impression.' A dependent culture is characterized by hierarchical control and a lack of participation. Decision-making is very centralized, employees follow orders and execute assignments, and personal decisions are only made after checking consultation with superiors.

Opposite to this are the development-focused and the self-actualization cultures, in which energy gets created and thrives. The development-focused culture is seen in organizations that are participatively managed and people-oriented. Members must be supportive and constructive and be open to the ideas and opinions of others. The self-actualization culture values creativity. Quality tops quantity; task fulfillment and personal development go hand in hand. Members are encouraged to enjoy their work, develop themselves and undertake new, interesting activities.

A different failure factor is the wrong mix in the type of 'followers' in a change. There are five types of followers[50] that can be distinguished:

- Alienated followers are critical and independent thinkers, but they are not prepared to actively participate in the groups to which they belong.
- Passive followers do not think critically or independently and also do not participate; they let the leaders do all the thinking.
- Conformist followers participate in their groups and organizations, but they are happy to do so based on orders and ideas of others, in particular those of the leaders.
- Exemplary followers are almost ideal as followers; they think critically and independently, take responsibility and really give their all; they actively participate in the group and organization.
- Pragmatic followers keep their options open, but also make the best of a bad bargain; they score average in terms of independent thinking and actively participating.

An excess of alienated followers, for example, can have a very negative impact on energy. A shortage in exemplary and pragmatic followers causes energy neither to be created nor to take hold.

In addition, the right form of leadership is essential for the right Energy. What is correct is determined by the type of employees or followers and by the type of change. Incorrect leadership is a failure factor *par excellence*. For example, coercive leadership, the giving of direct orders, while effective in crisis situations, in many other situations has a negative impact on climate and energy. Goleman[51] distinguishes six leadership styles in total, and posits that an effective leader must be able to use at least four of these six.

The six styles are:

- Coercive: the giving of direct orders ('do as I say').
- Authoritative: mobilizing people, starting from a clear vision and mission ('follow me').
- Affiliative: developing harmony and emotional connections and bonds ('people come first').
- Democratic: promoting consensus through participation ('what do you think of this?').
- Pacesetting: determining the pace and direction by maintaining high achievement standards ('do as I do, now').
- Coaching: developing individuals by counseling them and preparing them for the future ('try this for a change').

Effective leaders, especially those who are able to utilize the authoritative, democratic, affiliative and coaching styles, score the highest in positively influencing the climate and the results of the organization. Goleman links the question of how you choose the correct style of leadership to the type of change: the change situation and the change requirements. Coercive is especially effective in a crisis situation, at the start of a drastic reorganization and in the case of serious problems with employees that demand intervention. Authoritative is based on the creation of a new and appealing perspective and works in situations that call for vision and direction. Affiliative is a healing leadership style when there are rifts or traumas in a team or if there are stressful conditions. Democratic is particularly useful as a style when the issue at hand is to promote acceptance and input from valuable employees. Pacesetting is aimed at situations where an already motivated and competent team has to come up with results (even) faster. Coaching works especially in situations where employees do have the potential, but not yet the competency to deliver the requested achievements and therefore need assistance in doing so.

The styles also have different forms of overall impact on the organizational climate. This is the most positive with the authoritative style, and this impact is also positive with the affiliative, democratic and coaching styles. While useful in some situations, the coercive and pacesetting styles score negative in terms of overall impact on the organizational climate.

Near misses[52] constitute another failure factor within Energy. These are ideas or even strategies with potential that are developed at a lower level in the organization, but which do not come to fruition because they literally or figuratively do not reach top management. As a result, they also lack the necessary support. These strategies arise outside the formal processes, often in the periphery and sometimes even in the 'illegality' of the organization. They emerge spontaneously and out of a sharp focus on technology, clients and operational processes. To thrive, these strategies must be provided with energy at the right moment. If not, they will die off after a patient and isolated existence and the only residual is the frustration in the creators. The energy drains away or is cut off.

This also happens if failure factors such as inactive leadership, neglect of the social dimensions[53] of the change, deep-rooted values or loyalties are in play.[54] The same holds true for a negative relationship between the values associated with the change and with personal convictions.

A special failure factor in the area of Energy is associated with the so-called competing commitments. A competing commitment is a psychological dynamic that is 'visible' in individuals who show resistance during change—despite the fact that they have the ability to change, are very involved with the organization and genuinely support the change. Kegan and Laskow Lahey[55] consider this passivity as a form of personal immunity to change. The employees are in favor of the change, but they do not actually contribute to it because they are subconsciously afraid that it will erode another important or valuable commitment. An example of this is the postponing of imposed assignments (procrastination), because one is subconsciously afraid of being 'promoted away' from the group because of success.

Another factor that can frustrate Energy is learned helplessness.[56] This is a type of helplessness that is created when an organism is repeatedly exposed to harmful, unpleasant circumstances and there is no possibility of escape or avoidance. When this type of helplessness has settled in, not even escape routes that are offered will be used. People develop learned helplessness when they are exposed to uncontrollable negative consequences. People often initially react to such conditions with increased effort, to thereby try to regain control. But if that does not deliver a result, the learned helplessness is developed—resulting in a decrease in effort and activity in the future.[57]

Learned helplessness does not occur exclusively as the result of factors at an individual level; circumstances at group or organizational level can also lead to this. A high degree of routine in the work, autocratic leadership and a lack of autonomy, just to name a few, can cause learned helplessness and as such block the energy necessary for the change process.

Success Factors

Key success factors in relation to Energy are associated with the ability for change.[58] This pertains to factors such as change capability (knowledge and experience regarding change processes) and the availability of resources such as time, money, power, influence and position. But it also pertains to the awareness of change and consensus on strategic and change goals. Leadership, in particular in the form of emotional support and inspiration, is very important for the Energy needed to change. In this, Energy in a direct sense deals with enabling others to act and is as such a competence of effective leadership with the change.[59] Aside from this, four other competencies of effective leadership can be listed, bringing the total to five:

- Enabling others to act: creating conditions stemming from the belief in the potential and the capacities of the followers, so that people can achieve.
- Challenging the process: the continuous questioning of why things happen in the way they do or are done that way, and always asking for feedback on one's actions and ideas.
- Inspiring shared vision: involving and inspiring others by offering a vision on how the challenges can be approached and how progress can be made.
- Modeling the way: assuming the role of the exemplary model, 'show by doing' and act as a role model for change.
- Encouraging the heart: showing recognition and appreciation in a form that suits the needs and personality of each individual.

The other four parts primarily pertain to Effect (challenging the process), Rationale (inspiring shared vision), Focus (modeling the way) and Connection and Energy (encouraging the heart). This way each in its own way also influences the Energy for the change.

Katzenbach[60] describes what it is that change leaders do differently from 'regular' managers. What is important in this is that change leaders not only set high standards, but above all are involved with the question as to how to be able to mobilize and utilize the energy or capacities of their people as best as possible. This includes learning and experimenting. They work on creating a climate in which personal responsibility and space are combined with cooperation and support.

Appreciation is a key success factor in terms of Energy. Research by Bandura[61] shows that self-confidence, and not self-awareness, is the strongest predictor of the capacity to set ambitious goals, to persevere when there are setbacks, to be able to deal well with setbacks and also being able to actually realize goals. Hence, a success factor for Energy is strengthening the self-confidence of employees. Personalized appreciation is an essential component. Excessive self-confidence is countered by not only emphasizing one's own strength and feasibility, but to also point to the scope and degree of difficulty of the defined goals.

Heifetz and Laurie[62] provide principles for managing change. This explicitly pertains to the evoking, retaining and utilizing energy. A first principle or success factor is stress regulation: eliciting a productive amount of stress and maintaining this level in employees. There is a delicate balance between experiencing the need for change and becoming overwhelmed by it. The second principle is increasing responsibility and self-confidence: the development of a shared self-confidence. A management style of confidence emphasizes the personal responsibility of employees, instead of focusing too strongly on control. The last principle is protective leadership in the workplace: protecting employees who point out discrepancies in the organization. Leaders must resist their own tendency for rigidity and be open to potential, yet-to-be-discovered change opportunities.

According to Heifetz and Laurie, change management should focus on having people let go of the status quo and the creation of pressure. Research shows that letting go and developing pressure works more effectively if there is also much attention paid to the emotions and needs of the followers.[63] Effective change management combines a strong emotional focus on the change and much attention to the emotional needs of the followers: in other words, *warm* leadership.

CONNECTION

Connection plays a significant role in change in multiple ways as well as in the Change Competence Model. To begin with, this is about connecting Rationale and Effect to a change vision. In addition, the connection of

Focus and Energy to change capacity is important. Connection also makes the combination of change vision and change capacity productive. Management and solidarity ensure consistency and cohesion and, when connected with the other four core elements, obtain the optimal result from the change efforts. Strategy primarily connects to Rationale and Focus, consensus primarily to Rationale and Energy. Focus and Effect are connected by tasks, Energy and Effect by people. Change vision and change capacity and the four constituent factors are controlled, assembled and integrated by the change goals, change strategy and related change approaches and interventions.

Failure Factors

One of the first factors that hinder Connection is a lack of cohesion between the change goals and the actions needed to achieve them.[64] A second factor is that internal and external experts provide answers from their own expertise or area of responsibility. These are often one-sided answers. A third factor is formed by internal politics and divergent interests. This becomes visible in the form of narrow-mindedness, in problems at arriving at a collective action and in power struggles.

Sometimes the quantity and the speed of changes throw a monkey wrench in the works. The failure factor at Connection level in that case is pacesetting that possibly results in excessive change.[65] The willingness to change and the effectiveness decrease if the stakeholders consider the change(s) as excessive. This specifically occurs if the organization simultaneously implements different, incohesive or even conflicting changes. Duck illustrates this aptly with the following anecdote:

> One person's in charge of the root-canal job, someone else is setting the broken foot, another person is working on the displaced shoulder, and still another is getting rid of the gallstone. Each operation is a success, but the patient dies of shock.[66]

There is also excessive change if the organization implements new changes even before the previous change has been completed and evaluated, without giving the organization the necessary rest and time for business as usual and the capitalizing on the benefits.

Success Factors

The trick in change is to make it clear that, for every starting point—for example, a mission, organizational values or principles—discussion and action are necessary to give it value. If the trendsetters do this well, they can give direction to the change as the guiding coalition. A guiding coalition represents the right group of individuals, with the right characteristics and sufficient power and influence to be able to nurture and guide the change process. They help people to get along in an atmosphere of trust and emotional involvement.[67] If used properly, they are a key success factor in the change process.

All factors must contribute consistently and cohesively starting from the chosen direction of the change. There must be oversight and coordination, which often takes the form of good program management. Working systematically and methodically is very important to this program management. The fact is that research[68] shows that strategic, drastic changes benefit from such an approach. A good example of this is keeping Rationale, Effect, and Focus and Energy factors coherent. Bower[69] also calls this managing the systemic context.

Feedback is also an important component of a properly working Connection. Feedback must always serve toward the realization of the direction. This means that sometimes, in light of new information, adjustments may need to be made, and this requires feedback.

The Connection must also see to variation and diversity, which, according research by Abrahamson,[70] are important for a good change process. This pertains to dynamic change: important, radical change initiatives must be alternated with less radical, organic change. This way, after a radical change, the stability of the organization is enhanced so its energy can recover and the next changes can be processed more easily.

Another success factor at the level of Connection is effective communication. Research[71] shows that employees who feel that the communication about the change is of high quality are more open to the change itself. This relationship is influenced, however, by the degree of uncertainty associated with the change. In addition, trust in the sender plays a key role. The selection of the sender or communicator is a success factor all on its own. Communication about the change should preferably run through the direct supervisors.[72]

For some, the connection and coordination of the change invoke the image of a control tower. Hirschhorn[73] opts for the war room concept: a physical or virtual central space that handles the coordination of the change and helps to *"screen out many day-to-day organizational distractions."* This 'space' not only has a practical, but also a symbolic meaning. In this space, the conflicts and tensions, contradictions and potential trade-offs also come together—just like the confrontation between desirability and feasibility, change vision and change capacity, costs and yields, and opportunities and risks, all 'collect' there as well. The success factors that then count can be deduced, analogous to the requirements of an effective team.

Lencioni[74] associates productive cooperation or connection within teams with five functions:

- Trust;
- Conflict;

- Involvement;
- Responsibility;
- Results orientation.

If these do not work, or work incorrectly, they are dysfunctions. Each dysfunction is associated with a distraction, something that diverts the organization's attention from good cooperation. Figure 2.2 shows the dysfunctions and associated distractions as follows:

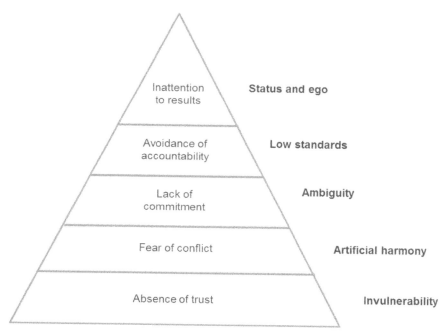

Figure 2.2 The five dysfunctions of teams (Lencioni, 2002)

The various dysfunctions and levels are interconnected. The first dysfunction is the lack of trust. This is 'solved' by showing that invulnerability is an illusion: people keep up appearances. In organizations that are effective, members trust each other at a fundamental, emotional level. Status and ego are subordinate to the collective. The vulnerability of the members (connected through their weak points, fears and errors) is not experienced as a problem because of that mutual trust.

That trust connects this first dysfunction with the second one: the fear of conflict. In an organization with sufficient trust, people do not avoid discussions that are essential for the organization. Individuals are not afraid of contradictory, conflicting points of view. On the contrary, these are seen as fuel for a sharp, passionate and fruitful dialogue. If such a basis of trust is lacking, the fear of conflict often dominates. Conflicts are avoided through a false and superficial form of harmony. This inhibits the aforementioned dialogue, which should lead to a sharp and shared image when it comes to dealing with critical issues and answers for the organization.

Superficial harmony forms the overture to the third dysfunction: a lack of commitment. Organizations that do enter into the conflict provide themselves with the chance to arrive at a truly shared and supported image. If not, what each stakeholder really thinks and wants remains unclear: the image of the *what* and *how* then remains ambiguous.

If the latter is the case, the fourth dysfunction is lying in wait: the avoidance of responsibility. In that case, what emerges are low demands of each other and poor follow-through and poor keeping of agreements and criteria.

This in turn leads to the fifth dysfunction: inattention to results. In organizations where individuals trust each other, dare to enter into conflict, commit to decisions and goals and hold each other responsible for them, personal agendas and individual interests will become subordinate to what is best for the organization. If an organization does not meet the stated conditions, this results in a lack of focus to collective results, and personal status and ego threaten to prevail. Connection is then a distant hope.

IN CONCLUSION

The five guiding factors and the underlying failure and success factors form dynamic combinations and patterns in complex change processes. We have illustrated with a large number of examples how they can help or hinder. The factors also show that it is a matter of customization, tailored to the specific context. Critical thinking is sometimes of vital importance for organizations to be able to change well. But sometimes it degenerates into dysfunctional smartness, and is an obstacle in the change process. Various factors and patterns emerge that are key or dominant in various contexts and subsequent phases of a change process. This dynamic is illustrated in the next chapter on the basis of a classic starting situation: a new leader taking office, who meets problems and challenges head on.

NOTES

1. Davis, S. M. (1984). *Managing corporate culture*. Cambridge, MA: Ballinger Publishing Company.
2. Van Witteloostuijn, A. (2003). Interview. In S. ten Have, & W. D. ten Have, *Het boek verandering*. Den haag, NL: SDU Uitgevers.
3. Argyris, C., & Schön, D. (1996). *Organizational learning II: Theory, method and practice*. Reading, MA: Madison-Wesley Publishing Company.
4. Dynamic conservatism is one of the four failure patterns distinguished by Argysris and Schon. Kloosterboer applies these to both the decision-making

about strategy and the exchange between strategy and execution: Kloosterboer, P. P. (2008). Navigeren bij strategievorming. *Tijdschrift voor Management & Organisatie, 5*, 5–22.

5. Van Witteloostuijn, A. (2003). Interview. In S. ten Have, & W. D. ten Have, *Het boek verandering*. Den Haag, NL: SDU Uitgevers.
6. Beer, M., & Eisenstat, R. A. (2000). The silent killers of strategy implementation and learning. *Sloan Management Review, 41 (4)*, 29–40.
7. Argyris, C., & Schön, D. (1996). *Organizational learning II: Theory, method and practice*. Reading, MA: Madison-Wesley Publishing Company.
8. Shanks, D. C., & Sommerlate, T. W. (1992). Envisioning: Creating the context for strategy. *Prism, Fourth Quarter*, 6–17.
9. Campbell, A., & Nash, L. L. (1992). *A sense of mission: Defining direction for the large corporation*. Reading, MA: Addison-Wesley Publishing Company.
10. Collins, J. C., & Porras, J. I. (1991). Organizational vision and visionary organizations. *California Management Review, 34 (1)*, 30–52.
11. Adamson, G., Pine, J., Van Steenhoven, T., & Kroupa, J. (2006). How storytelling can drive strategic change. *Strategy & Leadership, 34 (1)*, 36–41.
12. Ramanujam, V., Venkatraman, N., & Camillus, C. J. (1986). Multi-objective assessment of effectiveness of strategic planning: A discriminate analysis approach. *Academy of Management Journal, 29 (2)*, 347–372.
13. Podsakoff, P. M., Mackenzie, S. B., & Bommer, W. H. (1996). Transformational leader behavior and substitutes for leadership as determinants of employee satisfaction, commitment, trust, and organizational citizenship behaviors. *Journal of Management, 22*, 259–298.
14. Heifetz, R. A., & Laurie, D. L. (2001). The work of leadership. *Harvard Business Review, 79 (11)*, 131–141.
15. Beer, M., Eisenstat, R. A., & Spector, B. (1990). *The critical path to corporate renewal*. Boston, MA: Harvard Business School Press.
16. Schiemann, W. A., & Lingle, J. H. (1997). Seven greatest myths of measurement. *Management Review, 86 (5)*, 29–32.
17. Rousseau, D. M. (1995). *Psychological contracts in organizations: Understanding written and unwritten agreements*. Thousand Oaks, CA: Sage Publications.
18. Meyer, J. P., Allen, N. J., & Smith, C. A. (1993). Commitment to organizations and occupations: Extension and test of a three-component conceptualization. *Journal of Applied Psychology, 78*, 538–551.
19. Armenakis, A. A., Harris, S. G., & Mossholder, K. W. (1993). Creating readiness for organizational change. *Human Relations, 46 (6)*, 681–703.
20. Kuhl, J. (2000). The volitional basis of personality systems interaction theory: Applications in learning and treatment contexts. *International Journal of Educational Research, 33*, 665–703.
21. Rumelt, R. P. (1995). Inertia and transformation. In C. A. Montgomery (ed.), *Resource-bases and evolutionary theories of the firm* (pp. 101–132). Norwell, MA: Kluwer Academic Publishers.
22. McKinsey Global Survey Results. (2008). Creating organizational transformations. *McKinsey Quarterly, July*, 1–7. Acquired on March 19, 2013, via http://www.veruspartners.net/private/app/webroot/files/crog08.pdf.
23. Lewin, K. (1947). Frontiers in group dynamics. *Human Relations, 1*, 5–41.
24. Marks, M. L. (2006). Workplace recovery after mergers, acquisitions, and downsizings: Facilitating individual adaptation to major organizational transitions. *Organizational Dynamics, 35 (4)*, 384–399.
25. Pascale, R. T., & Sternin, J. (2005). Your companies secret change agents. *Harvard Business Review, 83 (5)*, 73–81.
26. Yukl, G., Guinan, P. L., & Soitolano, D. (1995). Influence tactics used for different objectives with subordinates, peers and superiors. *Group & Organization Management, 20 (3)*, 272–296.

27. Dickhout, R., Denham, M., & Blackwell, N. (1995). Designing change programs that won't cost your job. *McKinsey Quarterly, 4*, 101–116.
28. Kotter, J. P. (1996). *Leading change.* Boston, MA: Harvard Business School Press.
29. Harris, L. C., & Ogbonna, E. (2002). The unintended consequences of culture interventions: A study of unexpected outcomes. *British Journal of Management, 13*, 31–49.
30. Beer, M., & Eisenstat, R. A. (2000). The silent killers of strategy implementation and learning. *Sloan Management Review, 41 (4)*, 29–40.
31. Keuning, D. (2008). *Structuurhygiëne geboden.* Amsterdam, NL: Pearson Education Benelux.
32. Harris, L. C., & Ogbonna, E. (2002). The unintended consequences of culture interventions: A study of unexpected outcomes. *British Journal of Management, 13*, 31–49.
33. Schaffer, R., & Thomson, H. (1992). Successful change programs begin with results. *Harvard Business Review, 70 (1)*, 80–89.
34. Strebel, P. (1993). Het juiste veranderingsproces kiezen. *Holland Management Review, 37*, 112–118.
35. Davis, S. M. (1984). *Managing corporate culture.* Cambridge, MA: Ballinger Publishing Company.
36. Davis, S. M. (1984). *Managing corporate culture.* Cambridge, MA: Ballinger Publishing Company.
37. Hatch, M. J. (1993). The dynamics of organizational culture. *Academy of Management Review, 18*, 657–693.
38. Alvesson, M., & Spicer, A. (2012). A stupidity-based theory of organizations. *Journal of Management Studies, 49 (7)*, 1194–1220.
39. Goffee, R., & Jones, G. L. (2009). *Clever: Leading your smartest, most creative people.* Boston, MA: Harvard Business School Publishing.
40. Hill, A. (January 14, 2013). The quest for the right kind of stupidity. Acquired on June 20, 2013, via http://www.ft.com/intl/cms/s/0/2cefbab2–5b23–11e2–8d06–00144feab49a.html#axzz2blAGrCdP.
41. Meyer, R. D., Dalal, R. S., & Bonaccio, S. (2009). A meta-analytic investigation into the moderating effects of situational strength on the conscientiousness-performance relationship. *Journal of Organizational Behavior, 30*, 1077–1102.
42. Duck, J. D. (1993). Managing change: The art of balancing. *Harvard Business Review, 71 (6)*, 109–118.
43. Eisenhardt, K. M., & Sull, D. N. (2001). Strategy as simple rules. *Harvard Business Review, 79 (1)*, 106–116.
44. Mankins, M. C., & Steele, R. (2005). Turning great strategy into great performance. *Harvard Business Review, 83 (7/8)*, 64–72.
45. Neilson, G. L., & Pasternack, B. A. (2005). *Results: Keep what's good, fix what's wrong, and unlock great performance.* New York, NY: Crown Business.
46. Mankins, M. C., & Steele, R. (2005). Turning great strategy into great performance. *Harvard Business Review, 83 (7/8)*, 64–72.
47. Davis, S. M. (1984). *Managing corporate culture.* Cambridge, MA: Ballinger Publishing Company.
48. Senge, P. M. (1990). *The fifth discipline: The art & practice of the learning organization.* New York, NY: Doubleday Currency.
49. Deal, T., & Kennedy, A. (1982). *Corporate cultures: The rites and rituals of corporate life.* Reading, MA: Addison-Wesley Publishing Company.
50. Kelley, R. (1992). *The power of followership.* New York, NY: Doubleday.
51. Goleman, D. (2000). Leadership that gets results. *Harvard Business Review, 78 (2)*, 76–90.

52. Argyris, C., & Schön, D. (1996). *Organizational learning II: Theory, method and practice.* Reading, MA: Madison-Wesley Publishing Company.
53. Schalk, R., Campbell, J. W., & Freese, C. (1998). Change and employee behavior. *Leadership & Organization Development Journal, 19 (3),* 157–163.
54. Nemeth, C. J. (1997). Managing innovation when less is more. *California Management Review, 40 (1),* 59–74.
55. Kegan, R., & Laskow Lahey, L. (2001). The real reason people won't change. *Harvard Business Review, 79 (10),* 85–92.
56. Seligman, M. E. P. (1975). *Helplessness: On depression, development and death.* San Francisco, CA: Freeman.
57. Pittman, T. S. (1998). Motivation. In D. T. Gilbert, S. T. Fiske, & G. Lindzey (eds.), *The handbook of social psychology* (pp. 549–590). Boston, MA: McGraw-Hill.
58. Ghoshal, S., & Bartlett, C. A. (1996). Rebuilding behavioral context: A blueprint for corporate renewal. *Sloan Management Review, 37 (2),* 23–36.
59. Kouzes, M., & Posner, Z. (1998). *Encouraging the heart.* San Francisco, CA: Jossey-Bass.
60. Katzenbach, J. R. (1996). New roads to job opportunity: From middle manager to real change leader. *Strategy & Leadership, 24 (4),* 32–35.
61. Bandura, A. (1986). *Social foundations of thought and action: A social cognitive theory.* Englewood Cliffs, NJ: Prentice Hall.
62. Heifetz, R. A., & Laurie, D. L. (2001). The work of leadership. *Harvard Business Review, 79 (11),* 131–141.
63. Huy, Q. N. (2002). Emotional balancing of organizational continuity and radical change: The contribution of middle managers. *Administrative Science Quarterly, 47,* 31–69.
64. Beer, M., Eisenstat, R. A., & Spector, B. (1990). *The critical path to corporate renewal.* Boston, MA: Harvard Business School Press.
65. Stensaker, I., Falkenberg, J., Meyer, C. B., & Haueng, A. C. (2002). Excessive change: Coping mechanisms and consequences. *Organizational Dynamics, 31 (3),* 296–312.
66. Duck, J. D. (1993). Managing change: The art of balancing. *Harvard Business Review, 71 (6),* 109–118.
67. Kotter, J. P. (1996). *Leading change.* Boston, MA: Harvard Business School Press.
68. Calori, R., & Atamer, T. (1990). How French managers deal with radical change. *Long Range Planning, 23 (6),* 44–55.
69. Bower, J. L. (2000). The purpose of change: A commentary on Jensen and Senge. In M. Beer & N. Nohria (eds.), *Breaking the code of change* (pp. 83–95). Boston, MA: Harvard Business School Press.
70. Abrahamson, E. (2000). Change without pain. *Harvard Business Review, 78 (4),* 75–79.
71. Allen, J., Jimmieson, N. L., Bordia, P., & Irmer, B. E. (2007). Uncertainty during organizational change: Managing perceptions through communication. *Journal of Change Management, 7 (2),* 187–210.
72. Larkin, T. J., & Larkin, S. (1994). *Communicating change: Winning employee support for new business goals.* London, UK: McGraw-Hill.
73. Hirschhorn, L. (2002). Campaigning for change. *Harvard Business Review, 80 (7),* 98–104, p. 104.
74. Lencioni, P. (2002). *The five dysfunctions of a team. A leadership fable.* San Francisco, CA: Jossey-Bass.

3   Dynamic

Complex changes, and the processes associated with those changes, can take on various shapes and patterns. A merger has different requirements in terms of change management than does a reorganization. If the aim is a cultural change, different issues play a role than in a redesign of the organizational structure. In the following chapters, attention will be paid to the dysfunctions, leadership roles and change strategies and approaches and the situations within which they occur or to which they apply (in short, an overview and realization of diverging dynamics during change).

As a preparation for that more in-depth view, this chapter provides an outline of a possible dynamic: that of a new leader taking office, who meets problems and challenges with ambition. This will be done with a great amount of attention to the way change management can deal with 'taking office', using the factors Rationale, Effect, Focus, Energy and Connection.

It appears that in such a situation, leaders prefer to utilize the concept of 'the first one hundred days.' These form an important part of the dynamic to be outlined, as a beginning, but not as an end. The outlined dynamic is characterized by three phases: the first 100 days, the 265 subsequent days and the 365 days thereafter (i.e., the first one hundred days and beyond).

The central idea is that developing change requirements need changing leadership, changing leaders and interventions. During the first one hundred days, for example, different demands are made on leaders and different success and failure factors play a key role here than they do in the subsequent phases. Leadership must always and everywhere provide for a number of 'underlying functions' such as giving direction, offering protection and providing order. But in addition to this, depending on the phase and context of the change, specific contributions must be provided. An effective change in a well-performing organization demands a good and accentuated completion of the first one hundred days and the following phases. If the effective completion of the first one hundred days is missed, the following phases become more difficult. If the following phases are not completed well, the one hundred days benefit nothing. To prevent this from happening, it is important that the right topics and activities receive attention in the right phase. In addition, it is important that there be a clear direction, a consistent execution, cohesion and learning capacity across the phases. This starts and ends with the leadership: changing leaders must meet changing requirements for each phase.

Below we describe which three phases can be distinguished in a change project with the associated leadership development and success and failure factors. We then compare the three distinctive phases. This is accomplished with the aid of five success factors for leadership during change.

THE THREE PHASES FOR A NEW LEADER

The first one hundred days of a new leader form a recognized and useful label for the robust implementation of a change. They are the impetus to a recognizable dynamic. At the level of vision, mission and strategy, as well as organization and operation, there is generally much to be desired and to be wished for when taking office. Often, this arises from the necessity that is accented by acute problems such as poor financial performance, declining market share, dissatisfaction among the stakeholders, active and successful competitors or alternative providers and internal abuses. But often also from ambition, there is the honest desire to do things differently and better, to have ideas and insights that provide a better answer to the challenges and possibilities that external context and internal knowledge and skills offer. But it does not stop with those first one hundred days. Leadership and organization must continue afterwards. Once the course has been set and the 'honeymoon period,' the sensation of a new beginning and the 'planting time' has passed, there is still much that needs to be done. The organization must then actually change from the reorientation and the new direction and arrive at sustainable routines and behaviors as the basis for continuous improvement and sustainable success.[1] After the first phase of orienting (directing, redirecting), follow the phases of altering (changing the business) and leading (running the business). Each phase has its own questions and answers. These are described below.

Phase 1—One Hundred Days (100)

The tone is set during the first one hundred days. In terms of leadership, this revolves around forceful and strategic leadership. These two forms of leadership can be compared against facilitating and operational leadership.[2] It particularly deals with the creation and communication in outline form of the change case. This is particularly needed from the change leader who Katzenbach[3] compares against the 'regular' manager. Table 3.1 shows how and where these two types are different from each other. Although one looks better than the other, in a general sense it is not about right or wrong. In the context of the first one hundred days, however, it must revolve around the change leaders. In a more stable situation, elements that characterize the 'regular' manager will gain importance.

Table 3.1 Differences between a regular manager and a change leader (Katzenbach, 1996)

Key Issues	Traditional 'Good Manager'	Emerging Real Change Leader
Basic Mindset	Analyze, leverage, optimize, delegate, organize and control it	Do it, fix it, try it, change it— and do it all over again
	I know best	*No one person knows best*
'End-game' Assumptions	Earnings per share Market share Resource advantage Personal promotions	Value to customers, employees, and owners Customer loyalty Core skill advantage Personal growth
	Always make the numbers.	*Satisfy customers and workers.*
Leadership Philosophy	Strategy driven Decide, delegate, monitor, and review Spend time on important matters Leverage time	Aspiration driven Do real work Spend time on what matters to people Expand leadership capacity
	A few good men will get it done for me.	*I must get the best out of all my people.*
Sources of Productivity and Innovation	Investment turnover Superior technology Process control Leverage the people	Productivity People superiority Process innovation Develop the people
	People are an exploitable resource.	*People are a critical resource.*
Accountability Measures	Comprehensive measures across all areas Clear individual accountability	A few key measures in the most critical areas Individual and mutual accountability
	I hold you accountable.	*We hold ourselves accountable.*
Risk, Rewards, and Trade-Offs	Avoid failures and mistakes at all cost Rely on proven approaches Limit career risks Analyze until sure	Expect, learn from, and build on failures Try whatever appears promising Take career risks If in doubt, try and see
	I cannot afford to fail—or to leave.	*I can work here—or elsewhere.*

The leading question during this first phase is: What direction do you want to take as an organization? The answer comes in providing a vision, mission and game plan. To arrive at this, a good diagnosis of the situation (cultural framing) must be combined with a first draft of direction and organizational design (hard wiring[4]), during which the correct first messages and interventions are essential. These interventions often initially deal with difficult and hard topics: cost reductions, changes in the main structure and (more importantly) the associated responsibilities and authorities as well as the replacement of individuals in key positions. Ghoshal and Bartlett[5] call this the phase of rationalization. In the messages, the *heart* and *character* of the mission are the most important points of interest. The heart of the mission is about the *raison d'être*, the reason of the organization to be, in short: the purpose. Are the assumptions concerning that reason for being still valid and actual? Is the Theory of the Business[6] still valid, or is it outdated by changes in the situation (market, society, rules and legislation)? Are the associated business and mental models still/already correct, and do they still/already correspond?[7]

The character of the mission speaks to the type of mission: Is it a target, an enemy, a role model or a transformation?[8] For example, Walmart at the end of the 1970s implemented a major change with a target mission: double its own sales within four years to $1 billion. This kind of mission is motivating and stimulating, but also 'disappears' when the goal is realized. It is usually and especially suitable for the beginning and the first half of a change process. In addition to the type of mission, the described nature of the change and the communication style of the change agent are essential.[9] Are we talking about 'extensive maintenance'? Is the change agent a mechanic, or are we talking about the development and utilization of potential and is the change agent primarily a trainer and coach? From the perspective of the three phases, the message and the role must be correct. They can also vary through the phases (in conjunction): after a motivating enemy mission for the short term, a sustainable transformation mission for the long term; after the completion of extensive maintenance, a warm and motivating development process. In addition, these messages must touch individuals in the right way, thus not only cognitively but also and especially emotionally.[10] Many missions and related messages are technically well-defined, but do not elicit any reaction: "They imply a sense of direction, clarity of thinking, and unity that rarely exists."[11] This first phase must pay time and attention to this, but it does not become essential until the following phase.

The first signs of a sense of mission must be followed and realized by structure in a literal and figurative sense, but in particular in the purest sense of the word: that of a system of cooperation agreements. These form the translation of vision, mission and direction, or the core message for the change. They are the core elements of the game plan—the way in which the change is being approached. An important framework is formed in this by the types of simple rules: boundary rules, priority rules, how-to rules, timing rules, exit rules,[12] as introduced in the previous chapter. The first one hundred days are primarily about the first two types of rules. Boundary rules must ensure that individuals focus on the correct opportunities in the market or sector, and also describe what falls outside that scope. Priority rules aid managers in bringing order and setting priorities between goals, possibilities and requirements. This same function can, for example, be pre-eminently filled during the next phase by prioritized organizational values.

Phase 2—After the First One Hundred Days (+265)

In terms of time, the second phase covers more than double the time of the first phase. That first phase was dominated by a clinical, diagnostic view, and can also be described as primarily directive. The leadership style was a combination of forceful and strategic. In this second phase more space is created both literally and figuratively. The leadership orientation continues to be strategic, but is combined with a more facilitating rather than forceful style. The change leader continues to predominate, but must slowly but surely also be combined with the features and characteristics of a 'regular' manager, in person or within the top management team. The leading question now becomes: How can organization and behavior be changed in an inspiring and sustainable way?

Intellectually agreeing with each other about the mission and strategy (phase 1) is something very different from being ready emotionally and being committed (the task for phase 2). What must be present is a certain connection between the values and motivations at the level of the organization, groups and individuals: a sense of mission. The core of the answer to the leading questions above must be found in the development of the sense of mission and a set of supported change goals, along with a suitable change strategy. Often missions structured to be negative or compelling, such as the enemy and target mission, respectively, are not as effective during this phase as during the first phase. In the second phase, which changes from focusing to (actually) changing, what matters more are appealing goals and positive, inviting focal points in the form of a positive role model or a transformational mission, for example. What is important for leadership is exemplary behavior, close vicinity, attention and the language of the various target groups or followers.

The hard wiring must be followed by soft structuring: the preparing and helping the organization on its way by developing the changeability and creating or repairing the social foundation that must bear the change.[13] Where the first phase deals with rationalization, this phase deals with revitalization. Metaphors for leading and changing therefore move toward the direction of discovering and developing, guide and coach. The formulation and prioritization of organizational values is an important tool that makes the shift from predominantly directive to a more open and participatory style possible.

The most important simple rules are able to operate by the grace of the boundary and priority rules established in the previous phase: playing field and marching line are (until further notice, until the first learning experiences) clear. How-to rules describe which behavior and which operating processes are able to realize the mission and strategy and the therefore-necessary change. Timing rules ensure that people and divisions within the organization are in step with each other, are in tune and act jointly.

Phase 3—The Following Year (+365)

The first year of change, composed of two phases, is followed by the second complete year. This involves continuously improving or retrospecting: the systematic evaluation, interpretation and learning of the organization and its change and the associated context, mission, strategy, culture and structure. Business as usual, but then, thanks to the change, different. The leading question here is how to embed the change and advantages and to make them 'routine' in a way that ensures that the change rhythm and the (additional) change advantages are capitalized, preferably in a process of co-creation.

The leadership style now changes to a style that is dominated by facilitating and operational elements. Where necessary, forms of strong and strategic leadership, as part of continuous improvement and renewal, are added in. The answer to the leading question posed above lies herein: to shape the daily operations and planning and control and let them serve the formulated vision, mission and game plan: continuous improvement as a matter of course.

The most important simple rules in this phase are a synthesis of the rules from the previous two phases supplemented by exit rules. The exit rules aid in making decisions about terminating activities deployed and no longer pursuing certain strategic or change goals.

In this phase, the approach to changing has shifted from drastic and obvious to patching.[14] This means change management as proactive instruments, focused on changes that are usually small and sometimes somewhat larger and more radical.

Change is continual, ongoing: part, for example, of the 'normal' business operations, annual cycle and business processes. The change is also precise and concrete, and connected to one's own work.

FIVE SUCCESS FACTORS CUSTOMIZED BY PHASE

The question is what each phase should work on, what must be provided in order to be able to change effectively. As a framework, the elaborated set of five leading success factors (from Chapter 2) can be used: Rationale, Effect, Focus, Energy and Connection.[15]

The fleshing out of these five factors varies by phase. The success factors are further completed depending on the phase and pursuant to the stated leading questions and first answers. After this, the five factors are interpreted further, always starting with the elaboration and completion for the first one hundred days, followed by those for the other two phases. Table 3.2 gives an overview of the three different phases and their completion.

Table 3.2 The overview of the content of the three phases

Overview of the three phases	Phase 1: Provide direction (rationalize) (The first 100 days)	Phase 2: Changing (revitalizing) (The next 265 days)	Phase 3: Regular operational management (consolidating) (The next 365 days)
Rules	– Rules to make sure that employees know what is to be done (boundary) and when (prioritization)	– Instructional rules and rules for choosing the right timing	– New organizational and managerial rules – Deciding rules for terminating the pursued strategic or change goals
Agenda	– Arrive at a good diagnosis of the situation combined with a first draft of direction and organizational design	– Development of social foundation	– Evaluation and reflection
Leading questions	– Where does the organization want to go?	– How do you change an organization and its behavior in an inspiring and sustainable way?	– How are change and results to be embedded and 'made routine' in order for them to generate results in employees?
Decisive answers	– Having a vision, mission and action plan	– The development of a (feeling for) mission and change strategy	– Managing daily work activities and development – Planning and control based on vision and plan of approach – The creation of a culture that is tailored to continuous improvement
Rationale	– Provide a vision, mission and game plan – Provide strategic logic	– Becoming aware of goals and behaviors that represent what makes the difference	– Instilling the change logic, stories and overarching goals into the mindset of the organization

Overview of the three phases	Phase 1: Provide direction (rationalize) (The first 100 days)	Phase 2: Changing (revitalizing) (The next 265 days)	Phase 3: Regular operational management (consolidating) (The next 365 days)
	– The organizational and change story, meant for inspiration and motivation – Critical behavior specifications	– Creation of awareness, among others through change goals	
Effect	– Development of critical meta-performance indicators and a diagnostic feedback system – Catalyzing results	– Effort-appreciation-reward – Standards and values (control) system	– The organizational change must lead to new organizational routines and standards – Provide results – Kaizen approach: continuous, joint effort for (process) improvement – Development of boundary system for continuous identification of risks and threats – Learning through feedback about results
Focus	– Core business and organizational design – Non-negotiable minimum behavior – Core values	– Required behavior must be translated into systems and processes – Continued interpretation of goals to behavioral frameworks and personal assignments and testing these against dilemmas	– Continuous process improvement and evaluation – Permanent exemplary behavior

(*Continued*)

Table 3.2   (Continued)

Overview of the three phases	Phase 1: Provide direction (rationalize) (The first 100 days)	Phase 2: Changing (revitalizing) (The next 265 days)	Phase 3: Regular operational management (consolidating) (The next 365 days)
Energy	– Motivation and inspiration – Allocation of resources	– Claiming of resources – Servant leadership* – Placing claims on resources – Development of changeability * A style in which leaders operate and facilitate in the background instead of direct in the foreground	– Adequate resources management – Maintain behavior: keep repeating
Connection	– Overarching goals – Bringing entrepreneurship in line with the vision and mission of the organization – Connected leadership* * A style in which leaders can size up the formal organization and are able to engage the actual organization to attain the goals	– Personal leadership and connected leadership – Continuous monitoring of progress and, if necessary, adjust	– Tuning into and with each other – Sustainable evolution by development of the organization and persons in tune with each other

Rationale

The Rationale is about the idea behind the change, the strategic logic or reasoning, the story and the vision. The first one hundred days revolve around the vision and the business model of the organization. What is the story behind the change and the inviting perspective that is to inspire and connect? What is the purpose? What is the distinguishing capacity in terms of knowledge and skills, history and reputation, strategic assets and acquisitions that are to ensure a sustaining contribution?

In the second phase, the central question is what the gap is between the ambition described in the first phase and the current situation. What are the change goals and with what priority are they to be realized? What is their connection, are there synergies, dependencies or trade-offs? In this phase, mission and corporate story have to come to life and work; a sense of mission must be created. There, where the change goals pertain to the Rationale, the change goals must lead to a change of awareness, a feeling of collective ambition or experience of necessity. The goals and behavior must be given image and sound that will end up making the difference. What's it all about?

The third phase, the first complete year after, is about the instilling of the change logic, stories and overarching goals into the mindset of the organization.

Effect

What matters in Effect is that which counts and truly works in relationship to the change. The first one hundred days deal with the capacity for and daring to formulate meta-performance indicators. One example is the expression: "We do not compromise our quality." Another is Jack Welch's expression: "Fix it or sell it." The diagnostic feedback system[16] must start to come online, individuals must immediately know what is and what isn't appreciated and be able to act accordingly.

In the second phase this must be able to be converted to assignments and reasoning at the individual and group level. The trio of effort-performance-appreciation (reward) must be clear to everyone who needs or wishes to contribute to the change. The 'major' leadership based in the person of the top manager(s) must be combined with and slowly but surely make room for quiet leadership, desired behavior and self-initiative at an individual level. Management control depends on sharply formulated achievement indicators, but works through shared and prioritized organizational values that support daily behavior.

In the third phase, lessons and experiences must get set: new routines and standards must be developed. It is also clear what is not allowed and must be prevented; the boundary system identifies and addresses important risks and threats on a continual basis. The work style looks like the Kaizen approach: continuously reviewing together if it can be done differently and especially if it can be done better.

Focus

For focus, the first one hundred days revolve around core business and organizational design; what is the formula within which work is performed, and which organizational frameworks—structure, systems, processes and values—are part of that? It is essential to be able to formulate the non-negotiable minimum behavior derived from the Rationale: What must be done? What is (not) allowed?

During the second phase, the required behavior must be translated into systems and processes and, where necessary, into tasks, procedures and assignments. This is where the real behavioral change must be described and realized. Dilemma testing must outline answers where prioritization of organizational values still causes worries or causes lack of clarity.

In the third phase the optimization within frameworks, process improvement and continual checking and testing are the basis for focused action. Exemplary behavior and responsibility for individual behaviors with an explicit and recognizable relationship to Rationale and 'plan' are essential.

Energy

Energy means giving life to that which is desirable, against the background of the Rationale and keeping the Focus in mind. Who gets oxygen? Who is cut off? During the first one hundred days, top management also communicates by allocating the (best) people and resources or by 'withholding' the same.[17] Projects and departments as well as their budgets and teams are fed, enhanced or starved. The 'big story' of the first one hundred days is brought to life, with the correct tales, language and motivators.

During the second phase, a shift takes place from the allocation to the claiming of people and resources. People (must) support the consequences of the change. This revolves around showing and stimulating preparedness for change.

The third phase, running the organization or the regular operational management, revolves around good and (therefore) consistent and learning resource management; what is needed where, and how do priorities shift over time? What happens to the freed-up capacity? This is about maintaining the desired behavior, 'keep repeating' is the creed.

Connection

Connection during the first one hundred days is all about the higher purpose, preferably one that is also daring and manageable: the process-oriented answer to what binds and connects. Entrepreneurship in a form that is aligned, and leadership that is willing and able to connect (otherwise it's not leadership) is essential.

In the second phase, connecting means being able to convert the point on the horizon to behavioral frameworks, personal motivation and individual assignments and inspiration, in other words, deployment. This relates to 'personal' leadership, connected to and guided by the ambition or necessity for change formulated in the first one hundred days. The dream becomes a dream with a deadline.

This must continue during the third phase. This is about providing and continuing to learn, tuning into and with each other. Cohesion and organizational learning are essential. Organizational development and personal development must go hand in hand within limits to continue sustainable development and to prevent continuous improvement from remaining only an intention.

IN CONCLUSION

Dynamics, in terms of the requirements that are made by specific questions, contexts and phases, are examined in greater depth in the following chapters. In Chapter 4 we first pay attention to dysfunctions. These can cause dynamics, but also block dynamics. Understanding dysfunctions forms the basis for being able to indicate and handle (or break apart) wrong dynamics. Leadership plays a significant role in this. The diverging leadership roles can assist in approaching specific dysfunctions and the (renewed) dynamization of a change process. These are the topics of Chapter 5. Following this is Chapter 6, in which dynamics are crystallized with various change strategies and the combination of phases and approaches on which these are based.

NOTES

1. Ghoshal, S., & Bartlett, C. A. (1997). *The individualized corporation: A fundamentally new approach to management.* New York, NY: Harper Business.
2. Kaplan, R. E., & Kaiser, R. B. (2006). *The versatile leader: Make the most of your strengths without overdoing it.* San Francisco, CA: Pfeiffer.
3. Katzenbach, J. R. (1996). New roads to job opportunity: From middle manager to real change leader. *Strategy & Leadership, 24 (4)*, 32–35.
4. Bate, P., Kahn, R., & Pye, A. (2000). Towards a culturally sensitive approach to organization structuring: Where organization design meets organization development. *Organization Science, 11 (2)*, 197–211.
5. Ghoshal, S., & Bartlett, C. A. (1997). *The individualized corporation: A fundamentally new approach to management.* New York, NY: Harper Business.
6. Drucker, P. F. (1994). The theory of the business. *Harvard Business Review, 72 (5)*, 95–104.
7. Ten Have, S., Van der Eng, N., Ten Have, W. D., & Millenaar, L. (2011). Waarom businessmodellen zich zo moeilijk laten veranderen. *Holland Management Review, 137*, 53–58.
8. Collins, J. C., & Porras, J. I. (1991). Organizational vision and visionary organizations. *California Management Review, 34 (1)*, 30–52.
9. Marshak, R. J. (1990). Managing the metaphors of change. *Organizational Dynamics, 22*, 19–35.
10. Gardner, H. (2006). *Changing minds.* Boston, MA: Harvard Business School Press.
11. Campbell, A., & Nash, L. L. (1992). *A sense of mission: Defining direction for the large corporation.* Reading, MA: Addison-Wesley Publishing Company.
12. Eisenhardt, K. M., & Sull, D. N. (2001). Strategy as simple rules. *Harvard Business Review, 79 (1)*, 106–116.

13. Bate, P., Kahn, R., & Pye, A. (2000). Towards a culturally sensitive approach to organization structuring: Where organization design meets organization development. *Organization Science, 11 (2)*, 197–211.
14. Eisenhardt, K. M., & Brown, S. L. (1998). *Competing on the edge: Strategy as structured chaos*. Cambridge, MA: Harvard Business Press.
15. Ten Have, S., Ten Have, W. D., & Van der Eng, N. (2011). Veranderkracht: Vijf leidende slaagfactoren als brug naar doeltreffende verandering. *Holland Management Review, 135*, 16–24.
16. Simons, R. (1995). *Levers of control*. Boston, MA: Harvard Business Press.
17. Bower, J. L. (2000). The purpose of change: A commentary on Jensen and Senge. In M. Beer & N. Nohria (eds.), *Breaking the code of change* (pp. 83–95). Boston, MA: Harvard Business School Press.

4 Dysfunctions

The dynamic within organizations is tangible everywhere, in every location and at every level. Sometimes this can be positive, for example, when the organization has a new ambitious goal and people experience enthusiasm and renewed energy as a result. Sometimes the dynamic can also have a negative effect, and seriously harm the change success through symptoms such as being tired of and resistant to change. Instead of fighting these symptoms, management should learn to recognize the organizational dysfunctions that stand in the way of effective change, and be able to explain and address them.

When people want to explain successful or unsuccessful changes, they are often caught between two extremes: the one-dimensional perspective and the extensive complex of explanatory factors. The first often leads to explanations that are too simplistic. For example, 'the success of General Electric is the result of the leadership of Jack Welch'; or, 'the failure of Enron is the result of failing supervision.' The second, the extensive complex, leads to obscurity: a voluminous summary of symptoms of which it is difficult to make any sense. Both are not by definition incorrect. Sometimes success or failure is indeed largely determined by one factor, such as strategy or leadership. On the other hand, the disaster with the Herald of Free Enterprise ferry (in Chapter 7) can only be understood when a great many of factors, which jointly lead to the disaster, are taken into consideration.

In many cases however, the extremes do not help: in making the diagnosis and searching for solutions they easily lead to simplistic solutions (replace the leader), a lack of overview and insight, and 'trial and error' (we have to start somewhere). Not seldom they are the last convulsions of an organization before hard 'outside' (for example, by the holding company or external professionals) interference, often with drastic reorganizations as a result. It so happens that the previously mentioned 'solutions' seldom offer a way out if worse comes to worse: when radical change must occur and no mistakes are to be made.

Sometimes such solutions can be no more than fighting the symptom; the real cause is not removed. The symptom of the chronic cold can be taken as an example: if a cold were to be treated with a (nasal) spray to soothe sinus passages, there is a good possibility that it's about temporary relief. It does not, however, treat the real underlying problem or symptom, for example, an allergy.

Such syndromes also take place within organizations. People are often not aware of this, and indeed only treat the symptoms. This can work out all right, even for a longer period of time, but as soon as attention flags, those symptoms will return with a vengeance. Often those syndromes—or organizational dysfunctions—can also be seen during change processes: consistent configurations or 'forms' of problem areas. Those configurations provide a view of the connection between success and failure factors during change. But they also provide a view of possible tensions by exposing incongruences or inconsistencies in the change competence of an organization; for example, the mismatch between the change vision and the change capacity.

This chapter examines the question of which dysfunctions or syndromes can play a role when changing organizations. We will first examine what the nature and the role of syndromes are in changing organizations. Then the dysfunctions that are singular and twofold are addressed. We then explore which dysfunctions have an integral character and as a result 'affect' all petals of the Change Competence Model.

CHANGE COMPETENCE AND CHANGING ORGANIZATIONS

Dysfunctions often play a significant role in the lack of success of change projects. By focusing on the symptoms and leaving the underlying dysfunction untouched, the change competence of an organization is undermined.[1] Purely focusing on the (isolated) problem areas or symptoms is not totally strange; often those are immediately tangible and the most visible. Those painful areas can fall within one of the five petals, for example, an invariable low readiness for change (Energy) or changes that are watered down time after time (Effect). The causes can be located within the same petal. The cause of the low readiness for change can be due to a fundamental lack of knowledge about change processes (Energy) such that fear is created each and every time. Changes that cannot be anchored in the organization can be the result of wrong anchoring systems (Effect).

It is also possible that, although the pain is expressed in only one petal, the causes of the pain do not stay limited to that one petal. In that case, combinations must be considered; for example, the Rationale and Effect petals combination should be considered if there is a non-appealing vision for change, or the Focus and Energy petals, in case of insufficient change capacity.

Wherever the cause may be located, they each have a decreasing effect on the change competence of an organization. How high or well-developed that change competence must be, depends on the scope and complexity of the change to be enabled. A simple process improvement demands less of an organization than a complete transformation or strategic reorientation. Generally speaking, having an adequate change competence demands that

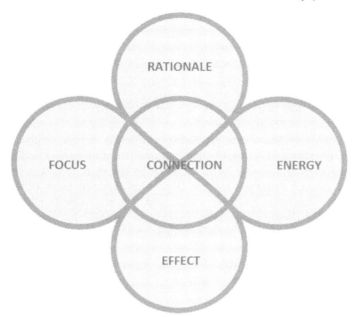

Figure 4.1 The Change Competence Model

the Rationale, Effect, Focus, Energy and Connection are well completed individually and cohesively and that they are correct (as far as content).

The idea is that the outer four petals (see Figure 4.1) must be completed at the desired qualitative level. If this is not the case, one or more organizational dysfunctions are created, or in other words, disruptions of the normal functioning of the change competence. The necessary cohesion between those four petals is created by the Connection petal, which must therefore be of a very high level. If the Connection is missing or has been incorrectly filled in, the model is out of balance. The change vision (Rationale + Effect), for example, 'demands too much' in regard to the available change capacity (Focus + Energy): change requirements versus change capacity. Such a dysfunction then explains why a change is not or cannot be realized.

SYNDROMES FOUND IN CHANGING ORGANIZATIONS

A syndrome is a clinical picture and stands for a number of (clinical) symptoms that always occur in combination with each other. In the context of an organization, the combination of such symptoms—just as the symptoms of a medical disease—can be the manifestation of an organizational clinical picture, syndrome or dysfunction. Kets de Vries and Miller,[2] for example, translate combinations of various organizational symptoms into five clinical pictures or syndromes: the paranoid, the obsessive-compulsive, the theatrical, the depressed and the schizophrenic organization. Each of these clinical pictures is characterized by a combination of specific symptoms. For example, the clinical picture of the paranoid organization is characterized by symptoms such as excessive monitoring, an inordinate amount of procedures, an extremely high number of control systems and a strong focus on planning. The effect of excessively 'scrutinizing' the environment and obsessively (wanting) to control internal processes goes without saying.

Such syndromes can create problems in times of change. A good diagnosis can help expose possible obstructing syndromes or dysfunctions. Such a diagnosis must preferably be made prior to the start, but if necessary, as soon as a change process that has been implemented faces obstructions. Sometimes a diagnosis has been made, but it is too superficial or limited. In this case the diagnosis remains limited to an isolated approach of the symptoms. An inadequate approach can result in the wrong selection of interventions, lead to inadequate results or can even worsen the clinical picture. Often all that is left then is fighting the symptoms and, in a best case scenario, temporary or partial relief.

ORGANIZATIONAL DYSFUNCTIONS

As previously described, dysfunctions can remain limited to the petal in which they are visible. In such singular dysfunctions, for example, there is a lack of sufficient Focus, the Energy is inadequate or a counterproductive Effect is being brought about. Two basic forms of singular dysfunctions can be distinguished: *absence* and an *incorrect* developed. In the first case, one or more factors within a petal are missing completely or have not been sufficiently completed: for example, there is no clear strategy and therefore no Focus. In the second case (incorrect developed) the factor has been incorrectly developed or counteractive to the advocated change. In this case, for example, not enough thought has been given to the redesign of certain processes (Focus) as a result of which they counteract the change instead of supporting it. As a result undesired behavior could be upheld. This is also called lack of alignment:[3] factors are incongruent in regard to each other or to the goal. A lack of alignment is also at play when, for example, the concerned parties do not accept the vision as part of the Rationale or the structure as part of the Focus—maybe because they are not able or willing to understand it, or just because they have a different opinion about the design, vision and priorities of the organization.

The next paragraph addresses the two types of dysfunctions (absent and incorrect developed) for each petal. For each dysfunction, examples of characteristic signs or symptoms are listed first and are then elaborated on. Often the characteristic signs are also (partial) explanations for the dysfunction and can be used to gain insight into possible useful interventions (in

Table 4.1 The singular dysfunctions

Condition / Petal	Absent	Characteristic symptoms (examples)	Incorrect	Characteristic symptoms (examples)
Rationale	Disoriented	- Inactive leadership - Strategic withholding - Short-sightedness	Disagreement	- Future shock - Inaccurate mission - Unidentified traumas - Illogical ambition
Effect	Disbenefited	- Lacking personal advantage (yield) - Unexperienced obligation - No personal sense of urgency - Chauvinistic conditioning - Fallacy of the exception	Disadvantaged	- (High) immediate costs of the change - Short-term thinking - Wrong information about or estimate of the consequences (negative perception)
Focus	Distracted	- Lacking exemplary behavior - Organizational silencing - No prioritized organizational values - Low modifiability (for example, due to nature of technology, lock-in by already made long-term investments)	Disapproved	- Ineffective, deeply rooted routines, ideology, institutionalism, homeostasis - Incorrectly designed prevailing circumstances such as reward systems and degree of autonomy
Energy	Disabled	- Capabilities gap - Individual inability - Limited change knowledge, skills and experience - Lack of budget and authorities - Lack of intellectual stimulation - Leadership behavior insufficiently supportive	Disengaged	- Reactive mindset - Cynicism - Breach of the psychological contract - Snow-blindness - Group-think - No awareness of change - Insufficient stimulation acceptance of group goals - Values not fitting the change
Connection	Disconnected	- Missing change plan and prioritization of strategic and change goals - Inadequate handling of dependencies, trade-offs, synergy possibilities	Disassembled	- Internal political and power struggle - Irreconcilable convictions - Emotional loyalty - Narrow-mindedness - Cannibalization costs - Lack of collective ambition - Separate rationalities
Context	Dissociated	- No eye for the external environment - Many missed opportunities - Time after time coming in 'second'	Organizational Attention Deficit Disorder	- Riddled external orientation - Excessive sensitivity for external stimuli - Easily distracted - Running hot and cold - Making choices is difficult (procrastination)

which, if the interventions are applied in a fragmented way, the risk of only fighting a symptom is always lying in wait).

Table 4.1 indicates per petal which dysfunctions are at play if the petal is absent (insufficient, limited or barely present) or is incorrectly developed. Characteristic symptoms are included as well.

SINGULAR DYSFUNCTIONS DURING CHANGE

Rationale

For the Rationale, the dysfunctions *Disoriented* and *Disagreement* are the dysfunctions when the petal is respectively absent and incorrectly developed. Disorientation has to do with characteristic and explanatory signs such as inactive leadership, strategic withholding and short-sightedness. Disagreement involves signs such as future shock, inaccurate mission, unidentified traumas and illogical ambitions.

Organizations that are disoriented lack direction. The cause is often a lack of leadership or a lack of strategy or even a combination of the two. Sometimes the disorientation is the result of introspection or short-sightedness. One example is organizations in the library field that first misjudged the changing role of information and communication in society, the possibilities offered by new technology and the changing behavior of consumers. Other examples are manufacturers of digital photograph frames that have been surpassed and superseded by tablets such as the iPad.

In the second dysfunction, Disagreement, the problem is not so much that it lacks leadership or vision, but above all that it is interpreted incorrectly by employees and other stakeholders. The 'troops' then find, for example, the outlined future too big and overwhelming and instead of inspiration and drive, fright and passivity enter in. The trick then is to again make the future manageable and digestible, for example, by outlining the path to that future and connecting it with the possibilities that employees do have or see (back-casting). Sometimes a lack of agreement is also due to an excess of assignments. This can be seen in the banking sector, where politics, external supervisors, new and old competitors, consumers and 'society' set a number of requirements that not only demand much, but are also sometimes at odds with each other.

Effect

The dysfunctions *Disbenefited* and *Disadvantaged* are central for Effect, the second component of the change vision. This first relates to characteristics such as lacking personal advantage (yield), important focus points that no one feels responsible for (obligation), no experience of personal need, chauvinistic conditioning and fallacy of the exception ('that does not work here'). Disadvantaged pertains to the (high) direct costs of the change, short-term thinking, incorrect information about, or estimate, of the consequences (negative perception).

With Disbenefited, individuals do not see their own or broader advantage or their own need for the change. Sometimes employees do understand the need for change from the Rationale and associated logic, but this is then a purely cognitive concept concerning the organization as a whole; they do not really *feel* the need for change and do not (yet) see the actual or anticipated consequences the change will have on them personally. What is often thought is that the announced change or outlined need concerns others. Then it does not 'touch' people. Sometimes this also involves overestimation of oneself (chauvinistic conditioning) and a too-brightly-colored a view of the (future) situation; or the idea that tried-and-tested change methods that have been attempted elsewhere will not work because their own group, department or organization is 'different' (fallacy of the exception) plays a role here as well.

In Disadvantaged, the second dysfunction, the problem is not that the change cannot be seen or that it cannot be estimated what it means or could mean; on the contrary, the change is estimated correctly in terms of value, but is evaluated as not (sufficiently) positive, rich in perspective or attainable from one's own point of view. Possible positive long-term effects lose out against comfort in the short run. The positive long-term effects can also lose out against direct costs of the change that are estimated too high, for example, in the form of a necessary move or a required training program. One often even has a negative estimate of the consequences that is sometimes based on perception or feeling rather than on facts. What helps in such a case is providing correct information, advice about the personal consequences in a positive and negative sense. Advice does not help, however, in situations where employees feel they are just not able to deal with the change, for example, due to a deficient level of training. In such a case they will have to be developed, and if that does not appear possible then a fair, business-like solution has to be sought out.

Focus

The dysfunctions at play in the Focus factor are *Distracted* and *Disapproved*. In the first case there are no leading frameworks that are guiding the organization. Characteristics include a lack of exemplary behavior, a lack of prioritized organizational values and a low modifiability of the organization (for example, due to the nature of the technology used by the organization and/or long-term investments already incurred and locked-in). An organization can also become distracted because of a structure that is too loose and voluntary. Characteristic for the Disapproved dysfunction are ineffective, deeply rooted routines, ideology, institutionalism or incorrect (developed) prevailing circumstances, such as reward systems and degree of autonomy.

Focus represents the reference framework and helps convert the *reason* (Rationale) for the change into a *direction* for the change. If this direction is lacking, the change is not or insufficiently guided and the organization is distracted. An adequate Focus helps the employees make the transition from the concept *that* something must happen to *what* must happen. Exemplary behavior as a basis for socialization and modeling is helpful in this process. The translation to the *what* does not work if, for example, no concrete indications for one's own actions can be derived from the organizational values. For this reason it is important not only to indicate that values and goals are important, but also what their prioritization should be.

In the second dysfunction, Disapproved, there is a framework, but it has been developed incorrectly noting the necessary change. Such frameworks are formed by, among others, deeply rooted routines and antiquated systems that stimulate and reward the wrong behavior in relationship to the desired change. The redesign of processes that do create cost reductions, for example, but infringes on the innovation capacity of the organization, is a type of wrong Focus. Another example is when placing the client central becomes important for a business, but the organization is designed such that employees are solely judged on financial targets.

Energy

The dysfunctions at play in the Energy factor are *Disabled* and *Disengaged*. Characteristics of the Disabled dysfunction include the capabilities gap, individual lack of capacity, limited knowledge about change, skills and experience, lack of funds, self-efficacy, intellectual stimulation and too little supportive leadership behavior. Clarifying and illustrative characteristics of the second dysfunction are a reactive mindset, cynicism and breach of a psychological contract.[4]

A disabled organization is 'switched off' in terms of capacity. It then lacks the necessary knowledge and experience, resources (time, money and authorities) and support to be able to play a meaningful role during the change (low readiness to change). It is possible that this 'only' takes place in the personal perception, but even then it has a paralyzing effect and robs it of the strength to be able to move. Being switched off as a result of absent leadership also occurs because management simply does not know how to activate the employees. An illogical allocation of resources can also drain the energy: crucial resources do not arrive at the correct location in time, which results in delays and loss of momentum.

The Energy can also be low as a result of the second dysfunction Disengaged. In that case, no one 'gets on board.' The change is then not experienced or embraced; no one is prepared to support the change (low preparedness to change). Often the causes are a cynical, helpless attitude toward changes due to previous negative experiences and keeping each other captive in old images and attitudes.

Connection

The singular dysfunctions *Disconnected* and *Disassembled* play a large role in the Connection. An important symptom with the first dysfunction is the lack of a change plan. If it is present at all, it often contains no more than the starting principles. It often lacks the prioritization of strategic goals and change goals. The result of the lack of such a plan is the inadequate handling of dependencies, trade-offs and synergy opportunities. In the second dysfunction, Disassembled, characteristic symptoms include internal politics and power struggle, irreconcilable convictions, emotional loyalty (holding on to the old for emotional reasons, not because it is still functional), narrow-mindedness and conflicting rationalities (for example, professionals versus management).

If an organization is disconnected, it is often unable to bring the change completely into being. It is possible that in first instance the motives for change (Rationale) are understood, what the ultimate target is (Effect), accompanying frameworks can be developed (Focus) and there is potential for movement (Energy), but it is not clear how everything is ultimately connected in order to get from point *a* to point *b*. A lack of knowledge about change management often plays a prominent role here.

An organization that is disassembled tunes all the petals individually, as a result of which they literally and figuratively all do 'their own thing.' This dysfunction is at play, for example, when, as in the previous example, several surgeries are taking place simultaneously that, when taken in isolation, are all successful but the patient dies from shock because the various surgeries have not been tuned to each other.[5] It lacks clear priorities, change logic and coordination mechanisms. It is not uncommon for this to occur as a result of a power struggle within the walls of the organization. It could happen that a business case for the change is created (Rationale), MD tracks are called into life (Energy) and processes are redesigned (Focus) without thoroughly being in tune with each other. This causes each part to break free from the whole and each starts to take on a life of its own. Each separate intervention no longer serves the higher purpose, instead each intervention serves individual interests. In those cases, central control is often lacking, but also order and connection between goals, possibilities and requirements, as a result of which the change does not get 'assembled correctly' or is not adequately managed.

Context

Chapter 1 added the possibility of a sixth factor to the model: Context. Not as failure or success factor, but more as the framework for the purposeful development of the other five factors.

Two dysfunctions play a role in the Context: *Dissociated* and *Organizational Attention Deficit Disorder*.[6] Characteristics of the first dysfunction include not seeing the external environment, many missed opportunities, consistently ending second. Characteristics that are part of the Organizational Attention Deficit Disorder dysfunction are a lack of a robust external focus, going along with trends (whichever way the wind blows), being extremely sensitive to external stimuli and procrastination.[7]

The Dissociated dysfunction has a particular character: the change competence of the organization is 'broken free' from the context and ends up 'outside,' as it were. The organization is then what it should be (in terms of internal consistency and cohesion of strategy, processes and leadership, culture and structure and sometimes even extremely well organized), but the model being used does not work, or no longer works, in the external context that has changed in the meantime. The organization is 'dissociated.' A good example is a mail delivery service that performs the traditional delivery of mail extremely well and is able to improve it, but simultaneously does not have an answer to the consumer nor a technology that demands and offers digital alternatives. In short, the Dissociated dysfunction holds on to or even perfects an organizational model that has already lost its role and meaning in and for the market—comparable to polishing the copper on the Titanic while the ship is already sinking.

Organizational Attention Deficit Disorder is the dysfunction taking place when the context is being utilized incorrectly. This dysfunction is also called over-sensitivity and is created when an organization has an extreme focus on its external orientation.[8] The organization then runs the risk of becoming like a feather in the wind; blowing in any which direction.[9] Contrary to the Dissociated dysfunction the organization does keep any eye on its external environment, but it is much too open to it. It is extremely sensitive to external stimuli: everything is interesting and everything is seen as an opportunity. The concentration span is short, which means that the organization is quickly distracted by irrelevant stimuli. This is similar to what is observed in children and adults who suffer from Attention Deficit Disorder (ADD). Among other things, they are overly sensitive to external impressions and are quickly distracted. As a result they have difficulty prioritizing thoughts and/or activities, because each stimulus is interesting or at least deserves attention. This expresses itself the same way in organizations: setting priorities is difficult, because setting priorities means keeping the attention on those issues that matter. Because there is no robust external focus, things are often postponed (procrastination)—making choices seems to be difficult. If choices are made, they are often based on that stimulus that penetrates best at that moment. Going along with (management) trends or organizing inspirational seminars without having thoroughly investigated what the added value for the organization is, are clear examples.

TWOFOLD DYSFUNCTIONS DURING CHANGE

Twofold dysfunctions always involve two of the five petals from the Change Competence Model. This can involve various combinations: vertical, horizontal and diagonal. The vertical axis pertains to the change vision (Rationale + Effect). The horizontal axis pertains to the change capacity (Focus + Energy). A diagonal dysfunction can exist, for example, in the combination of Rationale and Focus.

This dysfunction can again assume two basic forms in this combination. The first basic form is that the two involved factors are not in agreement with each other. For example, the Rationale preaches entrepreneurship through the vision, whereas the Focus barely offers the employees any room to develop their own initiatives through 'strict structures.' In the second basic form, the two involved factors are separated as a duo or deviate in regard to the 'rest' of the system. The Rationale and Focus factors, for example, are the instruments with which the board of an organization of professionals plans and develops profit maximization and a growth in sales, whereas

Table 4.2   The vertical and horizontal dysfunctions

Lemniscates	Dysfunction	Characteristics	Dysfunction	Characteristics
Change vision	Discomposed	Capacity without purpose	Disbelieved	Perceived 'false' pretenses
Change capacity	Disembodied	Purpose without capacity	Disordered	Lack of correct channeling of energy

the Energy, Connection and Effect factors emphasize personal growth and development for the individual professional. The syndrome at work here could also be referred to as the Ivory Tower.

The vertical and horizontal dysfunctions are discussed first (see Table 4.2).

Change Vision

Starting at the vertical axis or lemniscate, the change vision (Rationale + Effect), the dysfunctions *Discomposed* and *Disbelieved* play a role. The Discomposed dysfunction can occur when there is no vision for change. In that case, the answer to the modifications in the environment is missing; people don't know how to react to a new competitor, for instance, whereas experience has shown that the capacity is present to face even drastic changes.

In the Disbelieved dysfunction, the Rationale says something different than the Effect does to involved parties. For those involved parties (for example, the employees), it is a fact or a perception that their jobs are less secure, whereas the Rationale reflects a shining future.

Change Capacity

On the horizontal axis, the change capacity (Focus + Energy), the dysfunctions *Disembodied* and *Disordered* play a role. In the Disembodied, the capacity for change is insufficient or even absent in an absolute or relative sense, there is no 'body,' no system or capacity to bear the change. Due to the organization's rigid internal workings and the lack of Energy, the organization cannot 'process' the adjustments.

In Disordered, there is a sense of disorganization or 'disruption' of the change capacity; Focus and Energy are not connected to each other and have an unfavorable effect on each other. For example, when as a result of strong structures where there is hardly any room for own initiative, the Energy surely but slowly drains away.

DIAGONAL DYSFUNCTIONS DURING CHANGE

We primarily limit describing the diagonal dysfunctions to the two that do not mesh with the rest of the system (see Table 4.3). In total, four types of dysfunctions can be distinguished: *Ivory Tower, Collective Fantasy, Selfishness* and *Bureaucracy.*

The example of the Ivory Tower (Rationale + Focus) was given previously. The plans made in the ivory tower have a disturbing or confusing effect on everyone else. In the prior example (with maximization of profit as the goal) they stand counter to what is on the mind of professionals and what inspires them.

In Collective Fantasy, Rationale and Energy broke adrift together. A major vision, a daring goal or an inspiring example, kindle enthusiasm in the organization, but no one asks to what degree the conditions for being able to realize the dream or make the fantasy into a reality have been met.

In the case of Selfishness, Energy and Effect have together separated from the rest of the organization, which, seen from the collective, is of course bad, but sometimes it is at the very least understandable that it happens. This dysfunction can occur when, for example, a large consulting firm does a drastic reorganization, as a result of which the professionals seek their refuge on the outside with the client, get their energy there and measure their effect there.

In Bureaucracy, Focus and Effect have gone to live their own lives together. This dysfunction can be seen in organizations where performance management and performance indicators create their own world that deviates from what the organization ought to revolve around. It is more about holding accountable than about managing, more about meeting a standard than about performance.

Table 4.3   The diagonal dysfunctions

Petal	Dysfunction	Characteristics
Focus + Rationale	Ivory Tower	– The top is not related to the bottom – Often top-down initiated changes
Rationale + Energy	Collective Fantasy	– Major vision – Delusions of grandeur – Disturbed self-image – Unbridled energy in the wrong direction
Energy + Effect	Selfishness	– Egoistic – Individual 'focus areas'
Effect + Focus	Bureaucracy	– Strong sense of having to account for things – Choking monitoring systems

MULTIPLE DYSFUNCTIONS WITH AN INTEGRAL CHARACTER

In addition to the singular and twofold dysfunctions, a distinction could also be made for threefold dysfunction, but these are in most cases an inverse of a twofold dysfunction. In the case of the Ivory Tower, for example, in certain situations the problem maybe does not lie in the Rationale and Focus petals, but on the 'other side'—with the remaining three petals. The idea is good, but the rest of the system cannot process it or take it on in terms of Energy, Effect and Connection. In terms of content or strategy, it can make a big difference on which side of the 'medal' the problem is located. In the Ivory Tower example, the problem lies either with the Rationale and Focus or with Energy, Effect and Connection. After all, is the new strategy correct or not? In change management, however, this really matters less at first: the change competence is hampered regardless and the system is not working. Whether this is because of a wrong direction or lack of willingness or ability to execute the change does of course matter in terms of dealing with or treating the syndrome. A substantively incorrect course after all needs reconsideration and alternatives; the inability or lack of will to execute a change calls for the development of the necessary capacities, including working on the acceptance and commitment.

It can also be wrong across the board. An organization then battles a multiple dysfunction with an integral character—the change management system errors span the entire system. This always involves four or five factors, either individually or in joint interaction. These are the integral dysfunctions, and there are three possible ways in which they show up (see Table 4.4).[10]

Table 4.4 The integral dysfunctions (Van Witteloostuijn, 1992)

Dysfunction	Characteristics
Disruptive	– Various realities that oppose each other – running the business and changing the business fight for priority: the supporting forces of the past and the present are in competition with innovators and fresh blood – Control and change do not provide the necessary flexertion[1], adjustment and stability, but instead obstruct each other – Resource allocation and setting priorities have turned into a fickle process where one day the one and the next day the other gets priority ('wind vane') – Disorientation in managers and employees because they are not clear what to focus on - organizational confusion – Priority proliferation: everything is important (and as a result, nothing)
Disorganized	– Hesitation - lack of making decisions and taking action – No common vision - strategic withholding - lacking vision and direction – Lack of coordination (mechanisms) and guidance - daily battle because of lack of clarity about relationships - right of the strongest – No corporate story and/or compelling story
Disintegrated	– Decentralized units and individuals are going their own way, without positive supportive or correctional mechanisms – (Emotional) detachment: organizational sections and individuals are inundated, pull back - erosion of corporate citizenship – 'Civil war': groups and their convictions are fighting each other or divide the territory - no cooperation - inadequate attention to external environment and right to exist - own survival is at the top – Groups and individuals literally or figuratively say their goodbyes to the organization and society - pocket vetoes

The first integral dysfunction is *Disruptive* or disjointing—the connections are or are in the process of becoming broken. Internal opposing signals form, initially not because no work is being done on alignment, but because they are confronted with different internal and external signals. This dysfunction is sometimes the preparation for a fundamental change in the organization, a transformation in reaction to drastic changes in the market or technology. The second integral dysfunction is created because factors are not or only rudimentarily developed. Direction, frameworks, guidance and capacity are lacking: here the dysfunction *Disorganized* is at play. The organization lingers and procrastinates. We call the third integral dysfunction *Disintegrated*, dissolved or fallen apart. The organization moves on all sides, but lacks direction, connection and integration. Individuals leave or do what they themselves feel is important. There is a lack of communication and vital parts of the organization often literally or figuratively split off.

IN CONCLUSION

Adequate change competence is a deciding condition for being able to realize changes and the associated goals. Organizations must combine a guiding and appealing vision for change with adequate capacity for change. Factors such as the Rationale, Energy and Connection must therefore independently and jointly be in order. Here, perfection and the maximum are utopian. For management, also, and especially in situations of change, what is important is anticipating needs to an adequate or optimal degree, given the fact that resources are scarce: much has to be done, but not everything is possible. Disruptions are more the rule than the exception here due to conflicting interests, external impulses and changing needs, in addition to wear and tear and 'exhaustion,' for instance.

Sometimes disruptions can be prevented, but often that is not possible and the issue is one of restoring the balance, even if only for a moment. What counts here is that disruptions are not as important as getting back into balance. To be able to achieve that, it is important to discover, explain, categorize and address obstructions and their causes. This is why it is important to know and recognize dysfunctions during change. That helps in understanding the organization better. What does or does not work for this specific context and organization? How can it work or work better? What can be done to prevent dysfunctions from arising? This forms the basis for being able to talk about and work on obstructions and disruptions in change processes.

NOTES

1. Ten Have, S., Ten Have, W.D., & Van der Eng, N. (2011). Veranderkracht: Vijf leidende slaagfactoren als brug naar doeltreffende verandering. *Holland Management Review*, *135*, 16–24.

2. Kets de Vries, M. F. R., & Miller, D. (1997). *De neurotische organisatie: Irrationele onderstromingen van het management*. Amsterdam, NL: De Management-bibliotheek.
3. Daft, R. L., Murphy, J., & Willmott, H. (2010). *Organizational theory and design*. Andover, UK: Cengage Learning.
4. Rousseau, D. M. (1995). *Psychological contracts in organizations: Understanding written and unwritten agreements*. Thousand Oaks, CA: Sage Publications.
5. Duck, J. D. (1993). Managing change: The art of balancing. *Harvard Business Review, 71 (6)*, 109–118.
6. Motley, L. B. (2001). Coping with 'attention deficit'. *ABA Bank Marketing, 33 (8)*, 45.
7. Bohn, J. (2013). Overcoming organizational attention deficit disorder. Acquired on July 24, 2013, via www.slideshare.net/OEThinker/overcoming-organizational-attention-deficit-disorder.
8. Hardjono, T. W., & Ten Have, S. (1996). Het vierfasenmodel voor organisatieverbetering. *Holland Management Review, 46*, 12–18.
9. Ten Have, S., Ten Have, W. D., & Bour, A. P.M. (1998). *Organisatiebesturing: koers uitzetten en koers houden; Balanceren met strategie en prestatie-indicatoren*. Den Haag, NL: Elsevier Bedrijfsinformatie.
10. Van Witteloostuijn, A. (1992). Flexertie: Is flexibiliteit strategisch wenselijk? *Controller Vizier, 4*, 6–11.

5 Leadership

Leadership is crucial when changing, that isn't news to anyone. Good leadership requires, among other things, the ability to perceive and take advantage of the tensions associated with the variable and often contradictory requirements and needs inherent to changing and organizing. This requires that the determining factors for effective leadership are realized in a mutually cohesive approach. How these factors are realized is, and should be, different for each case: "one size does not fit all". Not only is every change process different, but even within the same change process there is often a need for multiple types of leadership. The component parts of such leadership profiles and the trade-offs, tensions, paradoxes or synergies that they create are an important topic in literature on leadership, organizing and changing.[1] When change or innovation is involved, the requirements are even higher; in fact, a unique set of leadership characteristics, behaviors or competences is required.[2] This is due to the varying requirements made in situations of change. Sometimes those requirements even oppose each other and, as a result, create tensions.

These tensions can take place at varying levels: at the individual, team, organization and context levels.[3] At the individual level, tensions may develop between evaluating and generating. Leaders are supposed to stimulate originality, out-of-the-box thinking and 'let a thousand flowers bloom,' while simultaneously be separating the wheat from the chaff and 'maintain the garden'.[4] The first (originality) requires stimulation and space, while the second (separating the wheat from the chaff) needs discipline and frameworks. If the first dominates, there is a threat of sprawl and anarchy. If the second dominates, originality is stifled and the learned helplessness enters into the picture. At the team level, there might be tension between limitations or boundaries and freedom.[5] Leaders must make time and resources available while also setting the tension and limitations needed for achievement. There is an important tension between creativity and efficiency at the organizational level—to stimulate creative thinking and keep costs low or at least under control. At the level of context, we can find an example of tension between feedback and rigidity. Organizations need to ask feedback from stakeholders on the one hand, but on the other hand the organization must avoid becoming enslaved or overly sensitive to the point where it lets itself be dictated to, which could cause it to lose track of its identity and course. Conversely, a company's own vision and results should not lead to myopia and complacency with the result that relevant developments in the market and society are missed, ignored or underestimated.

It is clear that much is demanded from leadership even just through these tensions. These requirements and tensions can be translated into types of leadership that are linked to the five petals and the Context factor of the Change Competence Model. Change, for example, is not possible when work is done at the level of Rationale, but not at the level of Effect: if there is only strategic, but no operational leadership. In this case there is a plan but no implementation. Strategic leadership is required from and for the Rationale, but for a change vision (Rationale *and* Effect), operational leadership is required as well.[6]

Another distinction between types of leadership is between the charismatic and architectural role.[7] The first type is strongly associated with Rationale and Energy. This role revolves around the transfer of a vision; to inspire and activate. The architectural role oversees the (broad outline) design of the organization. The second type is strongly associated with Rationale and Focus. There is an imbalance in leadership if the first has been provided for, but the second is absent or not aligned with it. The leadership in change processes would then lack a productive tension between and a fruitful mix of stimulating and dictating, charismatically and architecturally. Leadership that knows how to deal with tensions is called versatile leadership or balanced leadership.[8]

This chapter uses the Change Competence Model to show the main tensions that a leader needs to take into account when dealing with change.

LEADERSHIP ROLES DURING CHANGE

Balanced leadership means having the ability to cope with tensions and knowing how to turn these into fruitful combinations. Leadership must therefore be multifaceted; there is no such thing as *one size fits all*. Different tensions require different styles of leadership. A balanced combination of those different styles is essential to the ability of an organization to change. A balanced combination of styles requires a combination tailored to the specific situation, such that one style does not overshadow the other and that there is room for both the 'hard' and the 'soft'—sometimes parallel, at other times sequential. The different leadership styles reflect specific leadership roles that are crucial for successful change.

These roles can be visualized in the Change Competence Model (Figure 5.1). Each petal of the model has both hard (or 'cold') and soft (or 'warm') leadership roles. Both are necessary for the proper realization of each petal, and for the proper functioning of the overall competence of an organization to

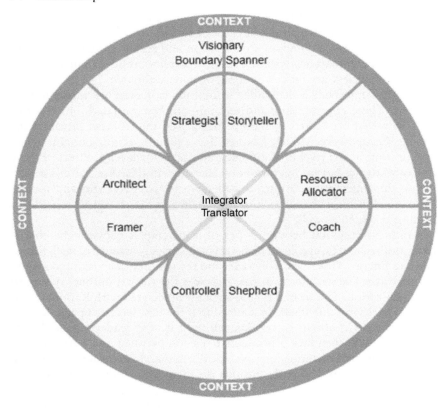

Figure 5.1   The twelve leadership roles

Table 5.1   The twelve hard and soft leadership roles

Petal	Leadership Role—Hard	Leadership Role—Soft
Rationale	Strategist	Storyteller
Effect	Controller	Shepherd
Focus	Architect	Framer
Energy	Resource Allocator	Coach
Connection	Translator	Integrator
Context	Boundary Spanner	Visionary

change. An overview of the twelve leadership roles and their classification as either hard or soft, is provided in Table 5.1.

Hard leadership roles primarily focus on the *what* of a change. They formulate the content of the direction of the organization, and work out the strategic logic: Do we globalize or not? Do we choose differentiation or not?

They also design the structures, systems and other frameworks and incentives that express choices and directions: Do we decentralize or not? Do we choose a reward system that is more individually or more collectively oriented?

The soft leadership roles are more focused on the *why* of a change. This brings the direction or the strategy to life and ensures that different people and groups within the organization are able to deal with it.

Antoine de Saint-Exupery expressed this combination of hard and soft— with a strong preference for the soft and warm: "If you want to build a ship, don't drum up the people to gather wood, divide the work and give orders. Instead, teach them to yearn for the vast and endless sea."[9]

The hard leadership roles provide the blueprints of the ship, the soft roles the dream, the expression of the longing for the sea. There must be a healthy, or rather productive, tension between the two kinds of roles: no motivation without a dream, no result without a blueprint.

Leadership in Rationale

For the Rationale—the reason for a change—the leadership roles are the *Strategist* and the *Storyteller*. The Strategist focuses in particular on the hard aspects such as the business case and strategic logic. The Storyteller takes care of the dream, the corporate story, mission or ambition: the soft. He brings the direction or the strategy to life and ensures that different people and groups within the organization are able to deal with it. The Strategist appeals to people with the what, the Storyteller with the why. The first is strongly cognitive and revolves around the ratio; it should add up and be understood. The second is strongly affective, involving emotion, its transfer, and allowing the dream to be lived.

An example of a great Strategist is Jack Welch, probably the most honored manager of the past decade. In order to get General Electric back on track, he introduced a simple, but not simplistic, strategic logic: *Fix it or sell it*. Faced with a very diversified and extensive global company in trouble, he gave his managers the task to become number one or two in its' own business in a relatively short period of time (fix it). Should that fail, their unit will be told farewell and divested (sell it). The rest is history.

The combination of the two leadership roles with respect to the Rationale, for example, was visible at the launch of Obama's health care reform plan in the United States. As a Strategist, helped by the best experts, policy makers and researchers in the field, Obama presented a sizable plan demonstrating the reason, desirability and feasibility. As a Storyteller, he brought the plan to life and made the motives visible and tangible. At the presentation, he had a child by his side that, due to inadequate health care, lack of availability and accessibility, had lost his mother. The Storyteller made it very clear: the plan is important, but this is what we are doing it for. Whereas the Strategist will and must rely on cognition and logic, the Storyteller needs to take care of the affective and emotional, the answer to the *why*.

Leadership in Effect

An important question for Effect is: 'What's in it for me?' Or, from the perspective of managerial and motivational theory: 'What makes Johnny run?' This involves the step from plan to implementation, from dream to action, where the rubber hits the road. Effect represents the actual or anticipated consequences of the change, the yield on organizational, group and individual level. For Effect, the core roles are those of *Controller* and the *Shepherd*.

The Controller is the one who is able to operationalize or concretize the Rationale. This leadership role ensures that employees are able to connect the larger and the smaller story. The Controller makes sure that the cause-and-effect relationships between effort, outcomes, reward and appreciation are clear and motivating for the groups and individuals involved in the change. The translation of the mission and organizational values into an action plan is just as important as the translation of the strategy and change goals into performance indicators and targets. The Controller focuses on behavioral patterns and dynamics and on concrete performance and numbers. This role also needs to ensure that the combined efforts and outcomes lead to the desired overall effect as defined by the Rationale. At the same time, however, the Controller must be able signal whether the Rationale is 'over-demanding' before or during the change process. If it is not possible, ambitions may have to be adjusted in terms of size or speed of the realization; or additional capacity (manpower, budget, knowledge) may have to be provided. The Controller makes these decisions based on facts and analyses.

The Shepherd can also fulfill a signaling function, but does this more based on intuition about groups and individuals. The Shepherd signals restlessness, confusion or disorientation and short-comings in a psychological sense. The focus here is not on monitoring and analysis, but on empathy, attention and knowing his or her people. This is an important task in the change process, because perceptions and feelings of those involved also, and sometimes especially, play a relevant and major role when implementing and sustaining change. It does happen that in spite of a cognitively and affectively sound and appealing Rationale, groups and individuals in the organization don't 'get on board.' This often happens because they perceive the consequence of the change as not positive or even negative (for themselves). This is due, for example, to the too-high experienced direct costs of change: people see the long-term benefits, but resist the short-term inconvenience, such as having to move soon.

Leadership in Focus

For Focus, the two leadership roles are the *Architect* and *Framer*. The Architect as the builder of the organization[10] is responsible for the structures, systems and procedures, but also for the prioritized organizational values and for strategy maps[11] to ensure that the *reason* for the change is converted into a *direction* for change. The point of engagement can be the individual and the system. The first uses programmatic change as a line of approach, and the second uses task alignment. In the former, the Architect will provide clear values as a basis for socialization. In the latter, the Architect will adjust the organizational structure or the process design in order to fit the change. The approach and the resulting interferences or interventions by the Architect are strongly focused on normalizing and dictating: ensuring compliance by providing clear frameworks.

The Framer, on the other hand, puts the ball in the court of the actors or those who are themselves involved, and develops processes that allow for the emergence of a shared meaning. Where the Strategist provides internal supply for the Architect from the Rationale, the Storyteller provides it for the Framer. Framing can be described as: "creating a point of reference against which some kind of action can emerge."[12] The primary goal is to develop a shared frame of reference together. The *reason* and the *direction* are developed during this process, and the selected course and goals for change are experienced. It is not the content statement as a formal structure or strategy that will serve as a guideline. It is primarily about the course of the process and the involvement of the stakeholders. Where the Architect serves to *push,* the Framer primarily serves to *pull.* Combined, these leadership roles strongly orchestrate the change.

Leadership in Energy

In the case of Energy, the leadership roles of the *Resource Allocator* and the *Coach* take central stage. Energy is understood as the fuel for change. In this analogy, the Architect is the driver of the locomotive of change, while the Resource Allocator and Coach are feeding the fire.

Bower[13] sees resource allocation as one of the most important functions in a change process. A change means a shift, and sometimes a ground-breaking shift in priorities. This cannot happen without consequences on the allocation of people and resources. Bower actually describes a variation to the saying "No money, no Swiss," or "No Energy (people and resources), no change." The Resource Allocator makes sure that the necessary resources for change are available: people, resources, time, money and attention. He has to provide these at the right time. Sometimes this includes a good 'purchase'— sometimes literally—of change knowledge, skills and experience.

The Coach ensures that the 'players' with their knowledge, experience and skills are placed where needed. He also contributes, like the Storyteller, to motivation and inspiration. The role of the Coach is that of active support: he must come into action if there are obstructions in relationship to the required Energy. This role must pay special attention to the capabilities gap, such as deficient self-efficacy, where employees feel ill-equipped for the change. However, the coach must also take action when a reactive mindset among employees threatens to throws a monkey wrench in the works. In those kinds of situations, he almost fulfills the role of a *mental* Coach.

Leadership in Connection

Connection involves the leadership roles of the *Translator* and the *Integrator*. The role of Translator is comparable to the role of liaison officer in the army. He ensures that the commands following from the chosen strategy and mission are communicated clearly and in a timely manner where they need to be. This leadership role is also responsible for a good connection or logistics between that what has been chosen to be the direction and framework, and the necessary resources. This role is actually a form of policy deployment: the translation of goals and frameworks to the deployment of resources and concrete assignments. In the context of change processes, this role is often at work in program management, with the accompanying image of the traffic tower or play director.

The Integrator focuses on cohesion, assessment and decision-making in the areas of dependencies, possible trade-offs and synergies. This leadership role provides the glue and oil to make sure that the components of the change process and their concomitant leadership roles work with and for each other, and prevents them from becoming isolated or counteractive to each other. It is the task of the Integrator to be specifically alert to internal politics and power struggles at the expense of higher goals. This also applies to incompatible beliefs among involved individuals and groups involved in the process, and a lack of a collective ambition serving as a basis for connection and coherence.

Leadership in Context

The sixth factor in the Change Competence Model is the Context. This involves the leadership roles of the *Boundary Spanner* and the *Visionary*. The Boundary Spanner controls which impulses, influences and information are retrieved from or allowed to enter from the environment. Too little connection to the environment or missing out on signals can be a matter of life or death for the organization. Developments in the market and in society won't be perceived, because the organization is not aware of it or lacks a frame of reference. This could be the result of the organization's navel-gazing, possibly as a result of previous successes. In situations of change, welcome, additional impulses for the change may be missed. The Strategist and Architect then miss crucial information and Rationale and Focus may be deprived or insufficiently supplied; however, if too much attention is paid to the environment (or allowed in) the organization is possibly hypersensitive and can drive itself crazy. Every move is perceived as an opportunity, each development is a reason to change.

The Visionary sees, feels *and* interprets what is happening in the environment and as such supplies important information to the Strategist and Storyteller, who can utilize his contributions to the Rationale. In order for this role to be effective for change, timing is essential. Visionary leaders often perceive needs, trends and patterns that others do not see. Apple's Steve Jobs is perhaps the best example. For their insights to 'come to fruition,' they can neither be too late nor too early. They should not be too far ahead of the troops when an outside insight or idea needs to take shape on the inside. If a vision is introduced too fast or if it is too grandiose, the organization may suffer from future shock: the image of the developments and the future is so overwhelming that it paralyzes rather than stimulates the organization.

DYSFUNCTIONAL LEADERSHIP PATTERNS DURING CHANGE

The effectiveness of leadership in change is highly dependent on the proper undertaking of the outlined roles such as those for the Storyteller and Resource Allocator. This involves the quality of each role, *as well as* mutual relationships between the roles as they relate to the specific context and to change. Dysfunctional leadership indicates that something is lacking within the individual roles, role combinations or their connection to situational requirements and needs.

The causes for this can be clarified by describing them as dysfunctions. Dysfunctional leadership patterns, just as the organizational dysfunctions described in Chapter 4, also consist of a number of (clinical) signs or symptoms, always occurring in conjunction with each other. The dysfunctions associated with leadership may be rooted in one of the petals of the Change Competence Model. For example, within the Context petal, the dysfunction *Organizational Attention Deficit Disorder* causes the Boundary Spanner not to set limits and the Visionary to be an eternal optimist: everything is perceived as an opportunity. The dysfunction *Dissociated* is another 'specific' dysfunction within the Context petal. The organization is detached from the context, (partly) due to inadequate performance or lack development of the Visionary and Boundary Spanner leadership roles (dissociated). The organization is cut off from its surroundings and unwittingly operates in a detached manner. It allows, for example, insufficient or wrong environmental signals, selects the wrong impulses from these signals or overlooks relevant ones. This can occur while other leadership roles function well, on their own, as well as in conjunction with other roles: a good organization, but in the wrong context. For example, IBM in the 1980s had an excellent organization for the mainframe market, but was blinded by its success and turned deaf. Their enslavement to the accompanying routines caused it to miss the rise of the personal computer with near fatal consequences.

Other dysfunctions may be related to multiple factors. There could be a strong vision for change, supported by the associated leadership roles, but there is also a dysfunction, because the necessary change capacity along with its required leadership is lacking or lagging. The Strategist, Storyteller, Translator and Shepherd then create a story that reflects and expresses the collective and the individual perspectives, but the Architect and Resource Allocator are not able to create a framework and the resources for the vision

for change to turn into results. Inadequate leadership causes the organization to be *disembodied* (see Chapter 4). This example shows a mismatch
between the change vision and the change capacity of an organization.

Diagonal Dysfunctions

Dysfunctions associated with diagonal petal combinations also exists. There
can, for example, be a problem between Rationale and Focus, or with them.
If there is a problem *with* the two of them, this means that they do not relate
to the other factors (or petals) of the model. The Strategist and Storyteller
(Rationale) have provided, in good collaboration with the Architect and
the Framer (Focus), a direction and a framework. If these are robust and
consistent, or even hermetic, a mental or organizational 'prison' may be the
result. The course and framework have then been designed 'somewhere at
the top' of the organization, but the top has, in the process, lost 'the rest.'
Counterweight and counterbalance are lacking or no longer used. This dysfunction can be called the Ivory Tower (see Chapter 4). The plans that have
been created in the ivory tower are disruptive or confusing to the rest of the
organization. For example, the leadership of a hospital with plans for the next
merger or sales growth has forgotten or is ignoring what drives the professionals. That would not have happened if the counterbalance of the Shepherd
had provided information about the experience, feelings, motivations and
emotions of the professionals.

Collective Fantasy is the second diagonal dysfunction. Rationale and Energy
together are adrift, and detached from reality, the opportunities, and priorities of the organization. Leadership roles such as those of the Storyteller and
Coach dominate and the organization may get carried away. It then lacks a
counterbalance from Focus and Effect. Leadership roles such as Architect and
Controller have provided too little or no discipline, review and prioritization.
In such a case, the productive tension is lacking, the power of the professionals
or top management dominates, and there is no opposing force that set limits.

Similarly, another dysfunction lurks when professionals and their immediate supervisors dominate, and there is no counterweight from leadership roles
related to Rationale and Focus. This dysfunction is called Selfishness (Energy
+ Effect). Professionals can, without limit, pursue their own goals and effects,
and spend their energy on whatever they choose to free it up for, including time
and budget. In this case, there has been no counterweight offered by the Architect using structures and systems, not through a collective ambition from the
Storyteller nor by the required interactions and 'translation programs' provided
by the Integrator and Translator to communicate and understand each other.

The fourth diagonal leadership dysfunction leads to Bureaucracy. The
organization has been 'boarded up' with rules and (monitoring) systems by
the Architect and Framer operating from Focus, and the Controller operating from Effect. Excessive management systems deprive the organization
of air for following its own initiative and experiments: everything has to

follow the rules, of which there are many. The soul of the organization is barely visible through the red tape. The Storyteller, Visionary and Integrator are not able to relate their vision or are not given the chance. The Resource Allocator acts as a slave of the bureaucracy.

Table 5.2 summarizes the four dysfunctional (diagonal) leadership patterns.

Table 5.2 The four/dysfunctional leadership patterns

Petals	Dysfunctions	Characteristics
Focus + Rationale	Ivory Tower	– Top is pipe-dreaming – Visionary, Strategist and Architect build impressively designed castles in the air – Top-down initiated changes that are not connected to moves, feelings and motivations of employees and other stakeholders – Shepherd is put offside or is underutilized – Controller and Translator cannot or do not want to do their jobs
Rationale + Energy	Collective Fantasy	– Grand, compelling vision, the sky is the limit – 'Going Hollywood' – Storyteller, Visionary and Coach bring organization into a higher atmosphere without moderation or correction, e.g. by Controller and Resource Allocator – Pride madness and distorted self-image – rampant, wrongly directed energy – Architect is not structuring – Shepherd lost his herd
Energy + Effect	Selfishness	– Selfishness and 'our own little shop' dominate because Storyteller and Strategist do not know how to formulate and convey a collective ambition – Coach and Shepherd are going 'native' and lose their leadership roles; become one with the group – co-workers focus on their own profit – Architect and Translator are not dictating
Effect + Focus	Bureaucracy	– Rules for the sake of having rules – lots of red tape – procedural, formal approach – strong emphasis on control and accountability – suffocating monitoring systems – Architect and Controller are supreme and have created their own reality – Management system is detached from vision, strategy, dream, and rationale for existence of the organization – Storyteller, Visionary and Integrator do not matter – Resource Allocator does not operate in line with vision and change goals; is, at best, slave of the bureaucracy

Integral Dysfunctions

In addition to the dysfunctions within one area such as the Context and the petal combinations, leadership may be dysfunctional across the board (integral). We call the first integral dysfunction *Disruptive*: The connections are or are being broken. Internally contradictory signals arise, not only because work on alignment is lacking but also because everyone is faced with different internal and external signals. The Boundary Spanner allows the wrong impulses in and ignores the good ones. The Visionary misinterprets. The Translator is not able to provide unambiguous instructions and gets confused, whereas the Integrator does not know how to connect the *what* and the *how*. This dysfunction is sometimes the prelude to a fundamental change in an organization, a transformation in response to radical changes in the market or technology. In other cases, this precedes a complete breakdown and the end of the organization.

The second integral dysfunction occurs when leadership roles have not been explicitly outlined or only rudimentarily. There is a lack of direction, frames, control and energy: there is a *Disorganized* system and a non-organized leadership profile. The leadership, whether singularly or collectively, delays, hesitates, lingers or procrastinates.

The third integral dysfunction is *Disintegrated*, dissolved or fallen apart. Leadership moves on all sides but lacks direction, connection and integration. And the organization, as a result, lacks these as well. People leave or they do what they think is important. There is a lack of communication and vital parts of the organization often split off, either literally or figuratively.

Table 5.3[14] gives an overview of the integral leadership dysfunctions and their characteristics.

ACTION STRATEGIES FOR LEADERS IN CHANGE PROCESSES

Looking at change and the competence to change from the perspective of leadership, we see that all roles need to be present, just as all petals—for example, Rationale and Energy—must be realized. But the interpretation of and relationship between the leadership roles will vary based on the context, the nature and extent of the change, as well as the characteristics of the organization. The twelve leadership roles can be used and realized in a variety of ways. They can be used for a diagnosis, the design, the anchoring and evaluation of change. They can be realized, for example, at different times and in different ways, with different people and/or different locations within the organization. Leadership roles related to the Rationale are usually filled at the top of the organization. But a leadership role like that of the Architect may suit the Chief Operations Officer very well. The role of Coach can be filled largely by the department heads, supported by HR. On the other hand, a role, for example that of the Visionary, may be important at the beginning or during the entire process of change, whereas a role like

Table 5.3 Integral dysfunctions and leadership roles (Van Witteloostuijin, 1992)

Dysfunction	Characteristics
Disruptive	– Due to the failure of various leadership roles, more specifically those of Integrator, Storyteller, Controller and Framer, there are different realities, and they contradict each other: running the business and changing the business fight for who comes first – the load-bearing forces of the past and the present are competing with innovators and 'fresh blood' – Control and change do not provide the necessary flexertion[1], adjustments and stability, but hinder each other – Visionary, Strategist and Integrator are experiencing conflict with the Architect, Controller and Resource Allocator, among others – Disorientation among managers and employees, because it is unclear what should be mobilized – organizational confusion – Priority proliferation develops because the Visionary and Strategist are not unambiguously supported by the Architect, Controller and Resource Allocator: everything is important (and therefore nothing is)
Disorganized	– Hesitation, lack of decision-making and action – Visionary and Boundary Spanner are not providing target scenario and information – Strategist and Storyteller cannot or will not take on their role. Result: no shared vision – strategic abstinence – lack of vision and direction – Architect, Framer and Resource Allocator cannot take up their role, because there is no Rationale and vision – Connection: lack of coordination (mechanisms) and leadership – daily struggle because of uncertainty about relationships – survival of the fittest
Disintegrated	– Integrator and Translator are failing to put flesh on the bones of a rationale for existence, a vision and strategy to use these as an unambiguous reference. Result: decentralized units and individuals draw their own plans without mechanisms positively reinforcing or correcting them – Failure specifically of the Storyteller, Framer and Coach leads to (emotional) detachment: organizational units and individuals are ducking, withdrawing – erosion of corporate citizenship – Shepherd is bordering on despair – Architect, Resource Allocator and Controller fail to provide organizational hygiene – Integrator and Framer don't provide cohesion and a shared frame of reference – 'civil war' – groups and their beliefs are incompatible with each other, or divide the territory – no cooperation – poor attention to the external environment and rationale for existence – one's own survival is primary goal – Shepherd, Coach and Integrator are unable to prevent that groups and individuals, literally or figuratively say goodbye to the organization and community – pocket vetoes

that of the Controller typically becomes more important during the later stages of the process.

In any case, in most large and more complex change processes, all roles need to be realized as such, in conjunction with and with an eye on the necessary productive tension. Generally speaking, these roles can be employed cohesively and productively using variations and combinations of *who* realizes them and with *what* and *how* and *when*. Different people, styles and competences, and various methods and techniques can be employed, either parallel or sequential. A multifaceted approach to effectively meet these needs and requirements is provided by Janssen and Steyaert.[15] They give a number of approaches to make fruitful use of dualities and tensions: sequencing, layering, interpenetration and reframing, among others.

Sequencing refers to a sequential or series of different leadership roles over the time. One or more specific roles are needed and dominant for each phase of a change process. It is easy to see that in the first phase, preceded by the preliminary work of the Visionary and the Boundary Spanner, the turn is to the Strategist and the Storyteller. At this stage they may also consult with the Resource Allocator and Controller to evaluate the feasibility of their vision and storyline. In the second phase, the step is taken from idea or main design to the development of the detailed design. Very likely, the Architect, Translator and Coach become more explicitly visible, supported by the Shepherd who keeps his pulse on the process, and the Integrator, who ensures that the old and the new, the ongoing and new initiatives, the change programs and the organization, are and stay interconnected. In a third phase, characterized, for example, by implementation, the Integrator and the Translator play a central role, actively supported by the Framer, Controller and the Resource Allocator. The Shepherd and the Coach are also, or especially, alert during this phase. Once the phase of business as usual starts, the roles of Controller and Resource Allocator may come forward, in which the accent on managerial and cyclic aspects predominates.

The second approach is layering, in which leadership roles are stacked, as it were, which gives them a more parallel and usually more collective character. Duck[16] is an advocate of layering, for reasons of efficacy and a good connection between planning and execution, content and process during change. She poses that dividing a change 'into pieces' does not work well. Top and bottom will then often operate separately from each other, practically or psychologically, due to a lack of consistency. The feasibility of the vision, acceptance and ownership are often weak spots. Duck emphasizes managing the dynamics and cohesion in a change process, in which interaction and balance between requirements and leadership roles are essential. A solution, according to Duck, can be to involve managers from the *entire* organization, or to let employees from all levels, high to low, participate from early on.

Another approach is the Transition Management Team (TMT). Duck indicates that this is a team that consists of eight to twelve qualified people involved in realizing the transition. They oversee the entire change process and provide direction, coherence, consistency and feedback. Everything that is needed is available, and the accents and roles within the team will be dynamical, depending on the situation, phase and change requirements. The team is a variation of the *Dirty Dozen*, a collection of knowledge, experience and skills or specialties with a strong connection between the constituent parts. The Visionary is already early on in contact with the Shepherd and the Framer, to ensure that the dream is converted into the correct imagery and impulses in order to prevent future shock. The CEO consults from the very beginning with the financial manager to ensure that their roles of Strategist and Resource Allocator contribute, at most, to only a small gap between desirability and feasibility. The Coach and the Architect ensure that a good 'setup' or 'field coverage' is combined with conjoint performance, delivery, learning and talent development. Sometimes layering is simply necessary to achieve effectiveness. The CEO as Visionary and Storyteller may launch the 'big story' in the early stages of a change process. However, the real communication needs to take place via the direct supervisor that is sensitive to and has knowledge of the primary process, the professionals and the clients.[17] These leaders take on the roles of Coach, Shepherd and Controller.

The third approach, interpenetration, focuses on breaking up the either-or approach that is often connected to duality. This approach can be seen as a radical way of acknowledging the *simultaneous* operation of both poles. In terms of change competence: Rationale is nothing without Effect; if Focus is lacking, Energy is wasted. In the field of change management, we have a similar dichotomy, which is the distinction between design and development. The interpenetration approach calls this 'developing while designing.'[18]

Another example in management science and communication studies is the distinction between top-down and bottom-up. Using interpenetration, the Japanese turn this into *Middle-Up-Down* management.[19] In terms of change competence, this means that parts and leadership roles are 'in conversation with each other' and strive toward synthesis. Key concepts are, for example, an '*Energetic* Focus' and an '*Effective* Rationale.' Leadership roles such as the Visionary and the Resource Allocator, or the Strategist and Coach, form (within the thinking and actions of an individual or team) a system of checks and balances and are able to leverage this tension productively at a higher level.

The fourth approach of Janssen and Steyaert is reframing. 'The third way' is a good model for this. It involves an alternative to two, usually opposing directions. Tony Blair has employed the term to find an alternative for the dichotomy between social-democratic and conservative-liberal viewpoints. A creative leap toward a third vision, direction or movement is required. Blair integrated two mainly social-democratic values (focus on community, equal opportunity development) with two conservative-liberal values (responsibility, mutual accountability of citizens and government). Reframing led Blair to the concept of CORA: Community, Opportunity, Responsibility and Accountability.

Another example of reframing is the Japanese concept of strategic localization. It breaks the deadlock in strategic and organizational thinking between economies of scale and local responsiveness.

The twelve roles when structured and applied in mutual relationship can be seen as a third way for leadership and change. Initial opposites such as desirability and feasibility, goals and resources, hard and soft, planning and implementation, and—according to some—leadership and management, do not disappear but are transformed into productive tension.

IN CONCLUSION

Many definitions of organizations and organizing focus on cooperation and mutuality as the basis for the realization of collective goals and common goals. At the same time, we see notions of diverging interests and rationalities, scarce resources and competing demands in organizing, such as efficiency and creativity. The latter are typically noticeable and often dominant in situations of change. They translate into competing requirements and demand much from leaders, whether in a team or other collective form. There is a need for direction as well as for space, for business decisions as well as for a sense of emotion; the organization needs a dream and a deadline, creative imagination and sobriety, scorching ambitions as well as good stewardship. Implicit conditions are survival, human scale and sufficient individual perspective. That's no sinecure.

These requirements can be translated into several crucial factors when facing major change, such as Focus, Connection and Energy. They are also reflected in the twelve different leadership roles and their relationships and mutualities. These roles become manageable and effective when their mutual tensions are correctly regulated during change. A lack of tension or stress leads to underperformance or nonperformance.

An excess of tension leads to mental or physical blocks, nervous exhaustion and poor performance. Productive leadership and organizing change require tension in the same way polar opposites need each other. One does not or barely exists without the other, and does not work, or works insufficiently, without the other. During changes, these requirements and roles create the necessary tension in individuals and organizations, they need to understand each other, complementation plays an important role, and they need to allow each other more or less space, depending on the context. For example, the vision and the Visionary need to challenge the organization and its employees without over demanding.

Organizations and their members usually do well with a healthy mix of change and more controlled periods and situations: dynamics and stability should alternate. In situations of change, the organization needs to function at a higher level of tension, which requires adrenaline. The 'organizational adrenaline' may be harmful in periods of stability, or lead to addiction if released in large quantities or for prolonged times. However, during change—whether out of necessity or because of ambition—adrenaline is welcome and even very necessary. Just as people create adrenalin when they suffer from anxiety, stress, or major threats or challenges, so should corporations when in similar circumstances. The adrenaline, the result of productive tensions between organization, change requirements and leadership roles, ensures that the organization is ready to respond. It creates preparedness and readiness, an organization that is awake, energetic and alert: an organization that is aware of its context, is focused and is ready to perform.

An example is the dual organization of the United States Army and the associated orientations and temperaments (or levels of organizational adrenaline). They have a model for peacetime and a model for war. During a war, tension increases, blood pressure rises and the adrenaline level goes up. Not too high, because that would create panic and hyperventilation. The Storyteller, supported by the Strategist, needs to provide an awake and driven organization. The Coach and Shepherd need to prevent employees from becoming too stressed out and starting to hyperventilate.

A healthy organization knows how to prevent, correct or compensate for dysfunctions using individual or collective leadership. This leadership provides that the organization can continue to perform, survive and grow while 'under tension' through good roles and mutual cohesive relationships. Such leadership is versatile or balanced. Balanced here means something different from always stable, let alone paralyzed (which is just as good as dead). Perhaps it is very often out of balance. Or: always searching and moving to find the right amount of tension. The real art is in regaining balance, again and again. If one succeeds, then tension and harmony are brothers in arms. Leaders who are able to accomplish this, maneuver like an old Japanese master who said: "I am very often out of balance, but I am also quick to find it back."

NOTES

1. Nasim, S., & Sushil. (2011). Revisiting organizational change: Exploring the paradox of managing continuity and change. *Journal of Change Management, 11 (2)*, 185–206.
2. Hunter, S. T., Thoroughgood, C. N., Myer, A. T., & Ligon, G. S. (2011). Paradoxes of leading innovative endeavors: Summary, solutions, and future directions. *Psychology of Aesthetics, Creativity, and the Arts, 5 (1)*, 54–66.
3. Hunter, S. T., Thoroughgood, C. N., Myer, A. T., & Ligon, G. S. (2011). Paradoxes of leading innovative endeavors: Summary, solutions, and future directions. *Psychology of Aesthetics, Creativity, and the Arts, 5 (1)*, 54–66.
4. Baer, J. (2003). Evaluative thinking, creativity, and task specificity: Separating wheat from chaff is not the same as finding needles in haystacks. In M. A. Runco (ed.), *Critical creative processes* (pp. 129–150). New York, NY: Hampton Press.
5. Mumford, M. D., Eubanks, D. L., & Murphy, S. T. (2007). Creating conditions for success: Best practices in leading for innovation. In J. A. Conger, & R. E. Riggio (eds.), *The practice of leader-ship: Developing the next generation of leaders* (pp. 129–149). San Francisco, CA: Jossey-Bass.
6. Kaplan, R. E., & Kaiser, R. B. (2003). Developing versatile leadership. *MIT Sloan Management Review, 44 (4)*, 19–26.
7. Kets de Vries, M. F. R. (2001). *The leadership mystique.* Upper Saddle River, NJ: Prentice Hall.
8. Kaplan, R. E., & Kaiser, R. B. (2003). Developing versatile leadership. *MIT Sloan Management Review, 44 (4)*, 19–26.
9. De Saint-Exupery, A. *If you want to build a ship.* Retrieved 19-01-15 from http://www.westegg.com/exupery/

10. Bower, J.L. (2000). The purpose of change: A commentary on Jensen and Senge. In M. Beer & N. Nohria (eds.), *Breaking the code of change* (pp. 83–95). Boston, MA: Harvard Business School Press.
11. Kaplan, R.S., & Norton, D. (2004). *Strategy maps: Converting intangible assets into tangible out-comes*. Boston, MA: Harvard Business School Press.
12. Smircich, L., & Morgan, G. (1982). Leadership: The management of meaning. *Journal of Applied Behavioral Science, 18 (3)*, 256–273.
13. Bower, J.L. (2000). The purpose of change: A commentary on Jensen and Senge. In M. Beer & N. Nohria (eds.), *Breaking the code of change* (pp. 83–95). Boston, MA: Harvard Business School Press.
14. Van Witteloostuijn, A. (1992). Flexertie: Is flexibiliteit strategisch wenselijk? *Controller Vizier, 4*, 6–11.
15. Janssen, M., & Steyaert, C. (1999). The world in two and a third way out? The concept of duality in organization theory and practice. *Scandinavian Journal of Management, 15*, 121–139.
16. Duck, J.D. (1993). Managing change: The art of balancing. *Harvard Business Review, 71 (6)*, 109–118.
17. Larkin, T.J., & Larkin, S. (1994). *Communicating change: Winning employee support for new business goals*. London, UK: McGraw-Hill.
18. Boonstra, J.J. (2000). *Lopen over water* (oratie, Universiteit van Amsterdam). Amsterdam, NL: Vossiuspers AUP.
19. Nonaka, I. (1988). Toward middle-up-down management. Accelerating information creation. *Sloan Management Review, 29 (3)*, 9–18.

6 Change Approaches

Previous chapters explained how successful change can be thwarted by dysfunctions or syndromes, and which leadership roles are required for change management to be effective. Many organizations in situations of change and faltering change management are doomed to trial and error—administering a pill without knowing the causes of the illness. At times their interventions are indicative of slavery to their routines and preferences. In addition, the sitting leadership is often more decisive for the chosen approach than required leadership, whereas it usually is more efficient and effective to choose and act based on a proper diagnosis. This highlights what the change goals are (or should be), and what dysfunctions are at play. Then the questions of what an appropriate change strategy might look like and which change approaches and leadership roles will help to implement these can be answered.

Change is not worthwhile if it is unnecessary, if a clear motive is absent. Change is not useful if it is done incorrectly. This leads, in both instances, to an incorrect scope of the change and its management. Because of limited knowledge, ingrained routines or near-sightedness, the reason for the change is misinterpreted. An adequate diagnosis is the solution. Reflection on the internal and external context, (change) history, current mission, ambitions and needs create a starting point. This way, the point of departure, reason and scope of the changes are brought into sharp focus. The *why* for the change gets shape and form. The effect of the change also needs to be clear: what should and will be the result of the change? Change can only be purposefully and deliberately assisted when this is all clear.

THEORY OF CHANGE

The limitations mentioned before, such as routines and personal preferences, not only interfere with the formulation of an effective change vision, but they can also negatively affect the change capacity. This is the case when one lapses into pigeonholing: the simplification of an issue, so it fits into an existing category with a corresponding solution. This leads to choosing approaches or interventions that one can handle or that have been applied successfully previously, rather than applicable ones.

A related shortcoming is the piecemeal syndrome, the tendency to tackle problems in the organization, or as an organization, in an isolated manner.[1] This often results in mere symptom control. One chooses, not hindered by a clear diagnosis, for traditional and emotion-based actions, which comes at the expense of rational actions with a deliberate balancing of objectives, resources and side effects. This can lead to collateral damage.[2] Purposive change requires and presupposes purposeful *and* effective action.[3] In the case of purposive, rational action, specific approaches are chosen, which are expected to contribute to the objectives. In some situations, the issue is not clear, let alone the goals. This requires creative search processes. In other situations, non-rational action is mostly unprofessional. It leads to wasted money, energy and health.

A Theory of Change[4] is useful for thoughtful design and development of change processes. This ensures that the required elements, factors and levels can be taken into account in a coherent and consistent way. The theory should then translate into a change strategy with associated approaches, interventions and conditions.

A Theory of Change comprises the following steps:

1. An observed change in the context appears to be relevant to the organization and is translated into a reason for organizational change and employee behavioral change.
2. The scope of the change is determined: Is it strategic or operational? Does it involve a part or the whole?
3. Based on this diagnosis, the change idea is formulated: What exactly is the problem? What are the options?
4. The change goals are formulated.
5. These change goals are the foundation on which a change strategy or overall plan can be built.
6. This plan then is the basis for a closer look at the most suitable and best-fitting change approaches to help shape the strategy.
7. The change approaches are the basis for interventions aimed at the organizational change and the behavior of employees to realize the change goals.

Within the Theory of Change, the change strategy and change approach play a central role. The two are inextricably linked: The change strategy is the overall description of how the change is to be realized. A change strategy is prepared in advance or develops over time into a coherent set of change approaches with associated interventions.

A change approach, in turn, is a specific method for the realization of (a part of) the change. The design of a change approach is done after the diagnosis, but they can also emerge in a more organic manner. Then, after evaluation a first approach will automatically lead to another (that strengthens, builds, corrects or compensates the preceding) and so on. Continuous and phased testing of the underlying assumptions, but also reflecting, evaluating and learning, will help you to develop a strategy that fits the situation.

In the case of relatively straightforward changes, the change strategy is simple as well, and a singular change approach often suffices. Relatively simple approaches sometimes require no more than one adequate intervention by which the change objectives are realized. For complex change issues, the strategy will be equally complex and multifaceted. Coordinated change approaches will then be deployed, in phases or sometimes at the same time.

In the medical world a same categorization (strategy—approach—intervention) can be seen when looking at the treatment plan of a patient. A treatment plan or treatment strategy is made up of one or multiple (depending on the illness or injury) approaches and accompanying interventions to combat or prevent a disease or injury. A treatment strategy for a heart attack may, for example, consist of three approaches, each with its own specific intervention (see Figure 6.1).

The first approach is of a surgical nature. The corresponding procedure angioplasty is used to eliminate immediate danger. This will pave the way for the second approach, which is the administering of hypertension medication. If, after some time, the heart has recovered sufficiently, the third phase may be used in parallel with the second. The third approach, physical therapy with cardio training as its intervention, is used to rehabilitate the heart muscle.

Obviously, the above-mentioned strategy concerns the main stages in the treatment plan of a heart attack. In addition to these main steps (which may differ in precise application per patient) patient-specific aspects also play a role in the treatment. Examples include dietary changes, structural exercise (after rehabilitation) and/or quitting smoking.

Sometimes when dealing with an illness, one can choose freely among approaches, and the order in which they are employed does not really

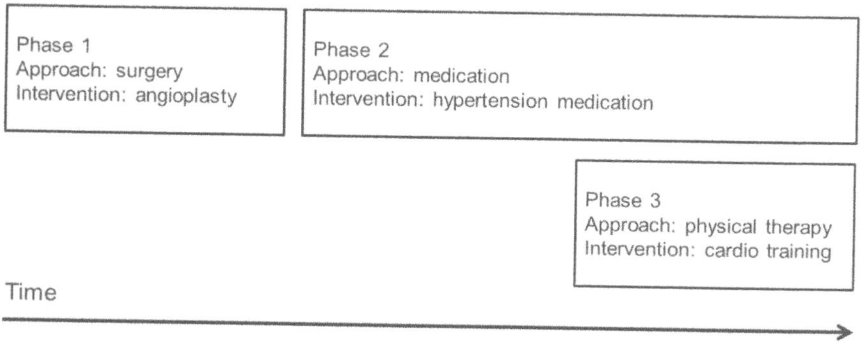

Phase 1
Approach: surgery
Intervention: angioplasty

Phase 2
Approach: medication
Intervention: hypertension medication

Phase 3
Approach: physical therapy
Intervention: cardio training

Time

Figure 6.1   Simplified schematic representation of a treatment strategy for a heart attack

matter. In these circumstances the strategy can take many forms. However, sometimes a more binding strategy is needed for a treatment to be effective. Which approaches are necessary depends upon the situation of the patient. The same is the case with changes in organizations: Sometimes change approaches are interchangeable, and sometimes there is a specific sequence of approaches needed to change successfully. Which approaches are necessary and in what order they should be used, also depends on the specific situation.

This chapter focuses on change approaches: Which ones can be distinguished and when are they used? In addition, we focus on examples of interventions related to the different approaches. We will conclude with some examples of change strategies based on the presented approaches.

A FRAMEWORK FOR CHANGE APPROACHES

The Change Competence Model (Figure 6.2) is the basis for different change approaches. A more complex purposive change generally requires a change strategy that integrates different change approaches. The Change Competence Model can distinguish between singular, diagonal, linear and integral approaches. The change requirements flowing from the change situation, and the organizational diagnosis that identifies determine what approach will be chosen. When a Rationale is lacking, for example, it will be a singular approach. The integral approaches focus on multiple change requirements with a comprehensive character: Rationale, Effect, Focus and Energy don't work together

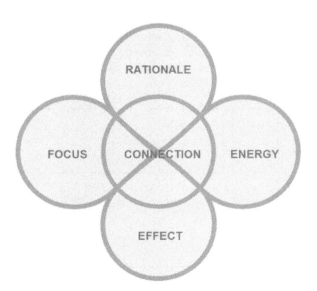

Figure 6.2   The Change Competence Model

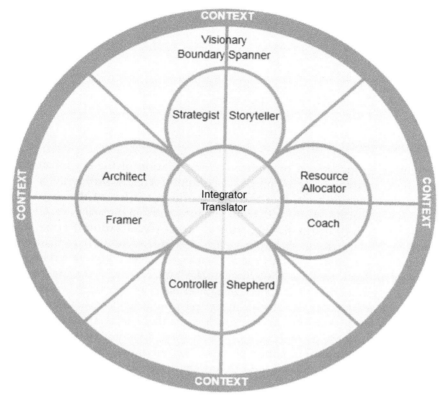

Figure 6.3   The twelve leadership roles

(properly). The approaches and interventions can be linked to the different leadership functions that play a role in change processes. Two leadership styles, a 'hard' and 'soft' one, can be distinguished for each of the 'five plus one' factors (Rationale, Effect, Focus, Energy, Connection, *plus* Context). For a Rationale, for example, both the Strategist (hard) and the Storyteller (soft) play a role. The first intervenes by formulating and presenting strategies, business models and analyses. The second mediates by conveying the corporate story, bringing ambitions to life and providing an experience of the missions.

   The twelve leadership roles are shown in Figure 6.3.

SINGULAR CHANGE APPROACHES

The six singular change approaches are: *Imagineering, Materializing, Containing, Fueling, Connecting* and *Regulating* (see Figure 6.4). These are discussed separately below.

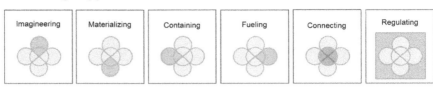

Figure 6.4   The singular change approaches

Imagineering (Rationale)

Imagineering focuses on the collective imagination of the organization's members. It involves developing and communicating a Rationale, a narrative that enables purposive and purposeful operation of the organization. Imagineering is derived from 'image' and 'engineering,' referring to the creation of a stimulating, fruitful target visualization. Formal and informal leaders are, in this approach, the engineers of an organization's capacity to imagine.[5] This approach focuses on developing the missing or incomplete Rationale for the change. The Strategist and the Storyteller interact to ensure that 'it' is sound. Imagineering as an approach is called for when a clear purpose[6] or *why*[7] (a higher purpose or collective ambition) is lacking. A lot depends on this approach when there are major and significant changes in the context of an organization. Existing views, routines, models and metaphors cannot be relied on anymore. Indeed, they are often a barrier and thus an additional challenge in shaping and implementing change.

For changes that are less drastic, Imagineering is no less important, but the effect is less dramatic. An example could be how a sound strategy is better expressed in an appealing vision. A more radical change (such as going from a manual to an automated process), or even a transformational change (such as the transition from a regulated monopoly to a competitive business) for example, requires more.[8] The organization must be led by the Boundary Spanner who manages the appropriate impulses, or it should be guided by the Visionary who offers and empowers new vistas. To be able to test the external impulses with the existing organization, both 'guides' need to do their work in close cooperation with the Strategist.

Materializing (Effect)

Materializing refers to the conversion of the Rationale into consequences, advantages and disadvantages, revenues and expenses, perceptions and estimates associated with the change for the various stakeholders in the organization. An employee may wonder, for example, how a forced relocation next year compares to long-term career opportunities.

This change approach aims to stimulate people to participate in the change. It is not the big picture but the small story that creates the point of action: What's in it for me (i.e., the individual employee)? This approach has a transformational as well as a transactional application. Interventions, in the first case, focus on norms, values and higher needs. In the second case, they focus on the exchange relationship by building appreciation and developmental opportunities into the change, for example.

Materializing may also focus either on more cognitive or on more affective aspects. An example of a 'cognitive focus' is providing personal targets or specific group goals along with work instructions that solidify the vision for change. The accompanying leadership role is that of the Controller. An example of an 'affective focus' is providing pointed education about the impact of the change in order to counterbalance perceptions, misconceptions and negative feelings. Identifying unrest and discontent and responding to it belongs to the leadership role of the Shepherd.

The literal meaning of materializing is 'to take a physical form.' In that respect, materializing is all about the continuation of the change effects, keeping them alive. It is about securing results and behavior in anchoring (reward) systems and policies that meet the organizational requirements, but who are also corresponding with employees' needs and wants arising from their norms and values.

Containing (Focus)

Bion (1897–1979), the British psychiatrist and expert in the field of group dynamics, viewed containment as the ability of parents to make complex or unbearable emotions manageable or tolerable for a child, thereby taking its intentions into account.[9] It is possible to contain in a similar way within the context of organizational change. For example, when setting priorities and explicating the values of the organization, employees are provided with the focus, framework and guidelines for making the change more manageable and tolerable. A clear organizational structure that is carefully translated to individual tasks also helps to contain the change by determining the degrees of freedom employees have. These provide employees with care, attention, safety and the overview needed to effectively deal with the change. Protection, comfort, security and care are provided to balance the fear and insecurity that come with organizational change.

In situations of organizational and behavioral change, that 'container' can be addressed in a similar way, for example, by a leader in the role of Framer and Architect providing an organizational environment in which change can be dealt with in a digestible and fruitful way. The leader contains through structures, the physical environment, systems and procedures, prioritized values and social support. An example that illustrates this comes from John Cottrell, president of the United Steelworkers of America. By channeling the organizational energy in the early nineties, he was able to increase productivity. He explained this by using the metaphor of molten steel. At United Steelworkers, employees work with potentially deadly powers. The essence of the business lies in the control of those forces. If that's not properly done then people could die. He argues that the same applies to people: People generate forces that can 'kill' each other. Like the melting cup that holds the energy of the molten steel, Cottrell argued, a container can hold and channel human energy productively without being destructive.[10]

A related perspective is the attachment theory of British psychiatrist Bowlby (1907–1990),[11] which is endorsed by De Wachter: "Man always wants to attach. That's because we are so desperately helpless when we are born. Put a child in the grass, a few hours later it's dead. An earthworm is born and is immediately an 'earthworm'."[12] Leaders must provide, analogous to the parent-child relationship, a secure attachment for those they lead. As a person, they offer a basis for exploring the new environment in situations of stress, uncertainty and change. Secure attachment requires a sensitive attitude on the part of leaders, respect for the autonomy of those they lead, and the support and structuring of the learning and change process for employees.

Fueling (Energy)

Fueling is the change approach when there's a lack of energy to change. This energy is the fuel that is necessary for a change. This involves both the 'softer' aspects of inspiration and (intrinsic) motivation, as the 'harder' components, such as budget, knowledge, skills and experience. Although inspiration is rarely underestimated as a factor for success, the same cannot be said for knowledge, experience and resources. Lack of the latter, however, called the 'capability gap,' is according to some researchers the second most important obstacle to change (deeply ingrained values come first).[13]

Bower considers resource allocation a key management process, because it operationalizes and solidifies the chosen direction and priorities.[14] Change involves new directions or priorities. This should have implications for resource allocation, to make new priorities visible and the related objectives feasible. The Resource Allocator, in addition to the Coach, is responsible for this approach. The Resource Allocator makes sure that people and resources are, and will be, in the right place. In collaboration with the Coach, the Resource Allocator also ensures that the composition of teams can be altered during the various stages or situations through the change process. Fueling as a change approach also implies that the Coach knows how to inspire and motivate on a more concrete level.

Connecting (Connection)

Connecting is the approach intended to bring relief when integral dysfunctions are an issue, for example, in the case of Disintegration. In this situation, a lot of things are happening in many areas, but coherence and consistency based on a chosen direction are lacking. It is the task of the Integrator in this situation to connect (e.g., by working on a collective ambition, collaboration and a common psychological contract).

Another example is disorganization: Potentially, there are a lot of insights and tools available, but the possibilities are not utilized, there is hesitation, and a lack of decision-making and action. It is the job of the Translator to connect and ensure coordination of content, formal coordination mechanisms, and management. The shared purpose, performance indicators, structures, systems, values and motivations, both at the level of individual employees and groups in the organization, all need to be reconnected.

Regulating (Context)

From a psychopathological viewpoint, regulating can be an approach to control an individual's exposure to (negative) stimuli. Influencing the external environment of the individual renders the often stressful influences manageable. This approach can also apply for organizations. It combines the concepts of stress and vulnerability, just like the vulnerability model of Zubin and Spring.[15] The Organizational Vulnerability Model[16] assumes that organizations have an innate vulnerability, and are subject to environmental factors and sources of stress that affect its functioning.[17] Vulnerability in a negative sense refers to hyper responsiveness, hypersensitivity and a reduced capacity to process information.

Stress sources include, for example, overstimulation and major occurrences, such as rapidly changing laws and regulations, the loss of an important customer, or the emergence of a new competitor. Dysfunction occurs when the relationship between the degree of vulnerability and the (perceived) amounts of stress is out of balance. This can be resolved by reducing vulnerability or influencing the quantity of stress.

Regulating involves: making stress or 'challengers' manageable.[18] It is possible to influence the objectified amount of stress or the perceived stress. The first (objectified amount of stress) can be achieved, for example, by influencing politicians to accelerate or delay legislation,[19] the latter (perceived stress) by 'gatekeeping' or modulating what becomes visible or noticeable to the organization—similarly to a bouncer who determines when visitors may enter an establishment. Through the regulation of information, the organization is shielded and protected, preventing an excess of impulses that would leave the organization unproductive.

Regulating, thus, is about the (passive) protection of the organization, but also about (active) influencing the environment (together boundary spanning). A good example of active influencing comes from Mark Zuckerberg, the founder of Facebook. He has formed a lobby group to influence national politics. One of his issues is to make certain laws less stringent, making it easier for American companies to attract and hold highly educated foreign talent.

Table 6.1 summarizes the singular change approaches and the associated leadership roles together and gives some examples of change interventions.

Table 6.1 Examples of singular change approaches and corresponding leadership roles and their interventions

Factor	Change	Leadership role	Interventions
Rationale	Imagineering	Strategist	Make strategic choices—design business model
		Storyteller	Develop corporate story—develop inspirational metaphors
Effect	Materializing	Controller	Define critical performance indicators—determine concrete goals on group and individual level
		Shepherd	Assess organizational climate—determine the desired freedom vs. safety ratio
Focus	Containing	Architect	To structure and design systems, develop set of behavioral guidelines.
		Framer	Describe and convey guiding organizational values—define exemplary role behavior and appoint role models
Energy	Fueling	Resource Allocator	Allocate resources like budgets, materials and people—gap analysis resources
		Coach	Assemble teams—coaching—develop skills—learn and stimulate appropriate behavior
Connection	Connecting	Translator	Connect higher goal, concrete targets and individuals motivators with each other—translating frameworks into people, behavior and resources
		Integrator	Strengthen cohesion and cooperation between functional areas and organizational units—connect spontaneous and planned change initiatives
Context	Regulating	Boundary Spanner	Lobbying—selecting information
		Visionary	Futuring—developing a vision

DIAGONAL CHANGE APPROACHES

Diagonal approaches are often used when the equilibrium or balance in the change process or in the organization is affected. If, for example, there was a combined development of a Rationale and Energy, there may well be a passionate and inspired organization with a dream, as well as an organization with an impaired 'change self-image.' The trick then is to keep the good, if necessary along with a correction or counterbalance. See Figure 6.5 for an overview of the four diagonal approaches.

Inspiring (Rationale + Energy)

The first diagonal approach is Inspiring. The combination of a Rationale and Energy provides relief to organizational change that suffers from a bureaucratized process. Program management, monitoring and planning dominate and stifle. The process is maintained by 'rewards and punishment' and depends on scores and results in smileys, heat maps, colors and stoplight charts. There is no soul in this kind of change processes; the *why* is unclear while dutifulness rules. A Rationale, combined with Energy, function to inspire, for example, by providing corporate stories and visions that touch employees. Inspiring, thus, is about bringing the change to life. Language (metaphors, myths, legends, and other types of stories) is of inestimable value.

Participating (Energy + Effect)

Inspiring is no solution when things go awry on a concrete level within the organization. The leadership 'dumps,' for example, from the ivory tower, the change over the rest of the organization: The Rationale and Focus have been carried too far. In this case it is important to involve staff and other stakeholders to counterbalance the Ivory Tower dysfunction. Participating is the best change approach, using Energy and Effect as the engine and engine oil. Based on their knowledge and experience of the business, employees need to be involved to achieve the best result.

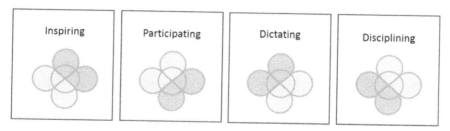

Figure 6.5 The diagonal change approaches

Dictating (Rationale + Focus)

When Energy and Effect are carried too far, selfishness starts to dominate. Anarchy and chaos emerge, and collective ambition, discipline and detachment are missing. The approach Dictating based on a Rationale and Focus will counterbalance this situation. The Strategist and the Architect in a collaborative effort will be able to create productive frameworks, and help define 'non-negotiable minimum behavior' as well as the degree of employee autonomy. Aligned with the change task and the organizational strategy, clear organizational frameworks are given that guide and direct the actions of employees. For example, when dictating the organizational core competencies, one framework could be: "This is what we are good at and therefore we'll focus on that." But also the operationalization of values of the organization and its prioritization ensure that behavior is directed toward the goals and again bear meaning and coherence.

Disciplining (Focus + Effect)

When Focus and Effect are combined, the change approach Disciplining is the result. Very specific and concrete frameworks, boundaries, direction and indicators are created. They result in deadlines, a base or bedding, and operationalization. This allows for testing of dreams, ambitions and visions. These clear frameworks also make it possible to reestablish management control. This change approach is also a necessary condition for being able to secure the change: Without discipline, employees will soon be doing 'other things.'

LINEAR CHANGE APPROACHES

The linear approaches involve the horizontal and vertical axis of the Change Competence Model (see Figure 6.6). They focus on the change capacity and the change vision. In a healthy situation they are in balance with each other. A problem exists if they are both underdeveloped with respect to what the organization, based on its assignment or mission, should perform or achieve. There is also a problem if one is insufficient compared to the other.

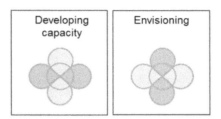

Figure 6.6   The linear change approaches

When this imbalance emerges the competence to change an organization is compromised. In the words of Bower: Purposive change[20] falters and there will be serious issues when trying to reconcile 'what it should be' with 'how it should be accomplished.'

Developing Capacity (Focus + Energy)

The 1984 Olympic Games in Los Angeles may serve as an example of Developing Capacity as a change approach. Just as with the Olympics in 1976 (Montreal) and 1980 (Moscow), the vision and mission were clear. The goal was to organize the best Games ever. However, whereas financial loss in Montreal and Moscow was an indicator of an inadequate capacity to change, something else happened in Los Angeles. The capacity to change was developed in such a way that it could responsibly and profitably cover the ambitions. New construction was limited to a swimming stadium and a velodrome, which were, in addition, paid for by sponsors.

Developing Capacity is an important change approach for missionary organizations and visionary leaders. They will often quickly and empathically unfold a powerful dream in such a way that it pulls the rest of the organization 'off balance.' The capacity to realize this dream must rapidly and adequately follow. The Architect and Framer should ensure that there is a sufficient Focus, and the Resource Allocator and Coach should prepare the "troops." If that isn't done properly, then the change vision is doomed.

Envisioning (Rationale + Effect)

The situation is different when it comes to the change approach of Envisioning. This is conceivable in the case of an organization that knows how to organize and is populated with mature professionals who possess the ability to self-criticize and reflect. Such an organization may be faced with motivated employees and managers who believe things *should* change, but do not have a collective or shared understanding of the *how*. Developing a collective ambition, a united vision and shared meanings, is at the core of the approach that must provide a counterbalance and a framework. The Strategist and Controller, together with the Storyteller and the Shepherd, must collaborate with the Integrator and the Translator, in order to provide a direction that resonates and appeals.

CHANGE STRATEGIES

More complex changes usually require more than a singular approach to be successful. To achieve solid and qualitative organizational change, a combination of approaches and interventions is therefore often needed. They should be coherent and consistent in form. This also needs to include an overall plan or change strategy. This strategy usually is the result of a well-thought-out design based on a proper diagnosis, learning experiences, and adjustments during the change process. Complex change processes are often characterized by diverging requirements, and usually also by needs that are at odds with each other. Decisiveness *and* support are necessary, as well as freedom *and* clarity, maturity *and* safety, a dream *and* a deadline, an attractive prospect *and* the agenda for next week, burning ambitions *and* a human dimension. The outlined change approaches offer solutions for all these needs and requirements.

The question is, however, in what order and what structure they should, may and are allowed to contribute. Sometimes a particular context enforces a specific approach as a starting point or a follow-up. A financial emergency requires above all Dictating and Disciplining—they can be thought of as a form of organizational first-aid. If fragmentation and conflicts in the organization are preventing change, Containing and Connecting are required. If employees don't feel heard following a first round with a well-sounding vision and tight plans, approaches such as Inspiring and Participating should balance this out. A powerful organization in a challenging environment with resilient employees will respond with Imagineering. Organizational climate and task maturity may sometimes make an obvious approach impossible, or a not-so-obvious approach feasible.

Sometimes, a situation requires multiple approaches. Sometimes they can be employed simultaneously, at other times a specific sequence is necessary. A combination of the two is also possible, but the situation determines its fruitfulness. The combination of all the approaches represents the change strategy. The change strategy can take on various forms. Different strategic combined approaches can be developed, depending on the requirements and needs of the internal and external context and existing possibilities. Using the change approaches outlined above, a number of example strategies will be given.

Example 1

Not much time is left for a professional service provider. The organization is plagued by a receding market share, acute financial problems, and selfishness among professionals. There is not much awareness of the need for change, but thanks to the presence of skilled professionals, there is potentially a capacity for change. Figure 6.7 shows the graphical representation of the chosen change strategy.

Central in the first stage is the change approach Materializing. Management and employees confront each other about the situation they are experiencing, the negative consequences, and the bleak future. The sense of urgency and the experienced need increase significantly; however, this does not decrease the business issues that are at hand.

The second phase initiates the change approach Disciplining. A non-negotiable minimum behavior is defined and made specific at an individual and

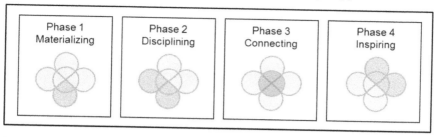

Figure 6.7   The change strategy for the service provider: 'From awareness to a new perspective'

group level. Frameworks and boundaries are established, and sharp agreements about results and behavior support a new psychological contract.

Once the organization has stabilized and moved out of the danger zone, a third phase begins. There is a need for a new vitality and a collective ambition. At the same time, there is awareness that any perspective will evaporate if nothing is done about the loose structure that still characterizes the organization. Old behaviors, temporarily suppressed by the high levels of distress, tend to come back. Old traumas and broken connections threaten to take their toll because there was no room to deal with them before. The third phase, therefore, starts with Connecting: Contact and attention are conditions that need to be met first.

The change approach of Inspiring follows next. The joining of a Rationale with Energy needs to do its work to heal the organization, and put it back in touch and balance with its context. The organization is changing not because of the past, but for the sake of the future.

The first example illustrates the creation of an awareness all the way to the inspiration of the troops giving them a collective ambition, a new perspective. It shows different requirements and needs that can be met over time in a succession of phases. This is the perspective of sequencing in which a strategy consists of a series of change approaches employed over time.[21]

Example 2

A large international technology group that also includes production units finds itself in heavy weather due to, among other things, declining government spending. The need to change is obvious to everyone, and quick action is required. Figure 6.8 represents the change strategy.

The first change approach is Dictating. The top level takes leadership with support and advice of external experts. New strategic principles are defined, as well as financial and operational criteria. They become the basis for 'simple rules,' by which strategy and direction are operationalized. These rules are utilized to include a review and a portfolio analysis, and lead to decisions to disinvest and disposes of a number of operations. The approach

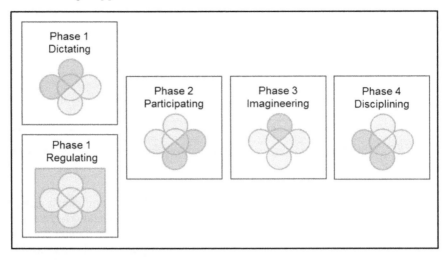

Figure 6.8   The change strategy for the technology group: 'Unleashing energy, creating return'

in this phase extends to the network of suppliers, which is also sorted out. Regulating, in this first phase, is an accompanying approach. Given the strong dependence on governments and their international policies, consultation is entered and lobbies are developed. This leads to clarity about the long(er) term orientation of key stakeholders outside the organization. It holds the opportunity to develop a long-term perspective, and limit or delay the short-term negative effects of the changing government policies. A side-effect of the choice to focus mainly on Dictating is an increased gap between top management, line managers, employees, among them a large number of highly experienced specialists, and the works council.

The primary focus in the next phase, therefore, is on the change approach Participating. Now that the company is 'cleaned up' and the acute threat has been removed, a dialogue is started to involve people in the change process, and to encourage them to contribute their insights and ideas for process improvements, for developing the organizational climate, and for technological and organizational innovations. This is a huge success, and a lot of energy surfaces 'naturally' with a tremendous level of commitment; it is raining ideas. Despite the simple rules introduced earlier, the organization, too soon, resembles the environment of a thousand blooming flowers in a poorly maintained garden. An evaluation brings to light that it suffers from a lack of a common target, a shared vision.

In the third phase, therefore, Imagineering is taken at hand toward the design of a shared and motivating purpose. Disciplining follows in the fourth phase to ensure a proper operationalization, which provides employees with hands and feet at their own level to realize 'the larger story.'

By disinvesting and disposing of a number of operations the organization frees up energy that can now be spend on core business activities. This change strategy also helps to achieve a 'high return on change investment' by creating a strong structure with accompanying systems en policies that focuses and facilitates every employee the right way.

Example 3

A south European utility company has a high ambition level coupled with a multitude of initiatives, but shows a lack of control. There is great political and union pressure on the leadership, and they point in conversations and in the media to an overload at management and staff level, and to what they view as disorder or chaos. The change strategy is visualized in Figure 6.9.

The change approach in the first phase of the change process is Containing. In response to the negative effects of the multitude of initiatives and the lack of overview, frameworks, limits and safety are provided for managers and employees. Action control and self-efficacy among many employees is positively influenced through combining clear criteria and priorities, and revising and highlighting processes and procedures. It also becomes clear again what has true priority and what is most important to deal with first. The priority proliferation where everything appears important is countered by resetting criteria and revising priorities. Once peace is restored, self-confidence and mutual trust are developing in a positive direction, and perspective is regained, phase two is initiated.

Discussions with stakeholders, including the unions, make clear that the ambition is largely endorsed, and the need to grow and develop is recognized.

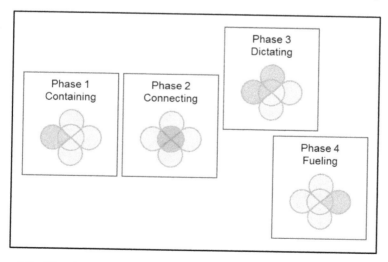

Figure 6.9   The change strategy for the south European utility company: 'From helplessness to a new self-confidence'

However, there is considerable criticism about the pace, the load, and the total lack of coordination. The organization was out of control. After the first phase with a focus on stabilizing, the real treatment or rehabilitation now needs to be initiated. Connecting is the approach. Using the prioritized criteria and trust as a basis, a global view and an integrated approach to the issues and challenges need to be developed. The criteria are validated with internal and external stakeholders, a dialogue is started, and order is furthered. All completed, ongoing and planned initiatives and projects are evaluated according to a mutually agreed framework. Some are stopped, while others are accelerated. Some yet untapped outcomes are now actually used, where possible, and projects and initiatives are combined or used in conjunction.

In the third phase, Dictating, the need for clarity and guidance is further met. Thanks to the trust and goodwill developed in the previous two phases, management can truly take charge again. Highlighting vision and strategy, and translating them into structures and systems after validating them with management and staff, make clear what the desired priorities and methods are.

The fourth phase, partially parallel to the third, is characterized by the approach Fueling. Budgets and other qualification are reallocated in line with the more specified and validated strategy. The necessary training will be provided, and some of the managers are replaced with people with the right kind of knowledge and experience relating to the strategy and new methods.

By clarifying the boundaries in conjunction with the enhancement of peoples self-efficacy an organization can avert from a situation where helplessness prevails and steer to a situation with a renewed self-confidence.

Example 4

A large company that provides various types of logistics has suffered some major setbacks. Two of the largest customers left, and a major bid project was lost to the nearest competitor. Figure 6.10 visualizes the chosen change strategy.

The change process is started with the approach Participating. A joint diagnostic process is started, involving eighty managers and direct supervisors and their teams. Using the method of appreciative inquiry (or humble inquiry), they assess areas of responsibility and customers. They map what they are good at and where they fail. They pay attention to customers, competitors, their own business operations, manners and style of operating, and the strategy that was defined two years prior.

The diagnosis and the displayed capacity for self-reflection and self-criticism, are used to develop a new vision in the second phase. The first stage had convinced them that things should be done differently, but did not know how. There was also a high degree of involvement and psychological maturity. Together, they aimed the search process toward a new vision. They developed scenarios and options and discussed strategic criteria. They achieved a lot in these areas. Many new, creative and promising opportunities opened up, but the collective choice process halted prematurely. Phase

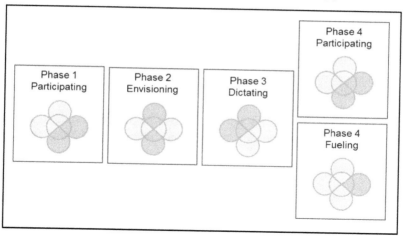

Figure 6.10   The change strategy for the logistics company: 'Turning shared vision into performance'

two was therefore wrapped up more quickly, and phase three was initiated with another approach.

The Board of Directors was provided with a third member who, unlike the two sitting members, had virtually no knowledge of the business. However, this former strategic consultant had over twenty-five years of experience in a variety of sectors and strategy processes. With him functioning as a pivoting point, the approach Dictating was developed. By making very selective use of internal and external expertise, the options were weighed and far-reaching choices made. One of the logistics businesses was sold, and the profits were used for two acquisitions and for autonomic growth of the retained businesses.

The latter was intensified in the fourth phase by using Participating and Fueling in parallel as change approaches. The existing knowledge, experience and vision were mobilized. Based on the highlights of the new Focus very specific investments were made in the remaining businesses and activities.

A joint diagnosis is essential for a widely supported change vision. By letting employees see for themselves what the current situation is, the organization can more easily and effectively formulate a vision for change. Once it is widely supported, dictating the necessary condition won't be met by unwavering opposition, especially when the softer side of change is sufficiently taken into account.

IN CONCLUSION

The change approaches based on the Change Competence Model contribute to a diverse set of strategies and tried-and-true interventions. They prevent change strategies from staying too abstract. They provide a handle for the overall plan for change. These approaches to change also prevent the selection of interventions from remaining a matter of trial-and-error (however valuable that sometimes might be). They also help ensure that interventions are conjunctively chosen and work well when used together. One intervention sometimes prepares the way for another; at other times it leads to side-effects or collateral damage. Sometimes, a subsequent intervention ensures that the benefits of an earlier one are solidified.

Change approaches are the building blocks of change strategies, and they effectively help in realizing an organization's mission, ambition, and other assignments.

NOTES

1. Skinner, W. (1984). *Manufacturing: The formidable competitive weapon*. New York, NY: Wiley.
2. Weber, M. (1947). *The theory of social and economic organization*. New York, NY: The Free Press.
3. Bower, J.L. (2000). The purpose of change: A commentary on Jensen and Senge. In M. Beer & N. Nohria (eds.), *Breaking the code of change* (pp. 83–95). Boston, MA: Harvard Business School Press.
4. Ten Have, S, Ten Have, W.D., & Janssen, B. (2009). *Het veranderboek: 70 vragen van managers over organisatieverandering*. Amsterdam, NL: Mediawerf.
5. Klaus, H. (1993). *Imagineren: Proces van (zelf)genezing*. Deventer, NL: Ankh-Hermes.
6. Mourkogiannis, N. (2006). *Purpose: The starting point of great companies*. New York, NY: Palgrave Macmillan.
7. Sinek, S. (2008). *Start with why*. London, UK: Penguin Books.
8. Marshak, R.J. (1990). Managing the metaphors of change. *Organizational Dynamics, 22*, 19–35.
9. Bion, W.R. (1967). *Second thoughts: Selected papers on psychoanalysis*. London, UK: William Heinemann Medical Books.
10. Senge, P., Scharmer, C.O., Jaworski, J., & Flowers, B.S. (2011). *Presence: Een ontdekkingsreis naar diepgaande verandering in mensen en organisaties*. Schoonhoven, NL: Academic Service.
11. Van IJzendoorn, M. H, Tavecchio, L. W.C., Goossens, F. A., & Vergeer, M. M. (1988). *Opvoeden in geborgenheid: Een kritische analyse van Bowlby's attachmenttheorie*. Deventer, NL: Van Loghum Slaterus.
12. De Wachter, D. (2011). *Borderline times: Het einde van de normaliteit*. Leuven, BE: Uitgeverij LannooCampus.
13. Pardo del Val, M., & Martinez Fuentes, C. (2003). Resistance to change: A literature review and empirical study. *Management Decision, 41 (2)*, 148–155.
14. Bower, J.L. (2000). The purpose of change: A commentary on Jensen and Senge. In M. Beer & N. Nohria (eds.), *Breaking the code of change* (pp. 83–95). Boston, MA: Harvard Business School Press.
15. Zubin. J., & Spring, B. (1977). Vulnerability: A new view of schizophrenia. *Journal of Abnormal Psychology, 86*, 103–126.
16. Van Dis, D., Hermon, A., Slomp, M., & De Vos, R. (2009). *Issue paper on terrorism*. Retrieved on 01-07-2015 from: http://www.erim.eur.nl/fileadmin/default/content/erim/research/centres/scope/research/issue_papers/state_-_civil_society/terrorism%20(2009).pdf

17. Compare: Nuechterlein, K. H., & Dawson, M. E. (1984). Psychophysiological dysfunctions in the developmental course of schizophrenic disorders. *Schizophrenia Bulletin, 10 (2)*, 204–234.
18. Zubin. J., & Spring, B. (1977). Vulnerability: A new view of schizophrenia. *Journal of Abnormal Psychology, 86*, 103–126.
19. Pfeffer, J., & Salancik, G. (1978). *The external control of organizations: A resource dependence perspective*. New York: Harper & Row.
20. Bower, J. L. (2000). The purpose of change: A commentary on Jensen and Senge. In M. Beer & N. Nohria (eds.), *Breaking the code of change* (pp. 83–95). Boston, MA: Harvard Business School Press.
21. Janssen, M., & Steyaert, C. (1999). The world in two and a third way out? The concept of duality in organization theory and practice. *Scandinavian Journal of Management, 15 (2)*, 121–139.

7 The Change Case—Part I

The Board of Directors (Board) of a large international company gets together at the beginning of December. A meeting with the Supervisory Board is planned for in two weeks' time; a meeting that needs to be prepared for. In the past year, the development of the organization and the improvement of the results have been prioritized, but unfortunately without the desired result. Despite a number of large projects and interventions, the results are downright bad. There is a lot of unrest and the organization's image and reputation are deteriorating.

The Board's Chairman wonders how this is possible. So many actions have been taken; so many changes have been carried through. Yet no progress has been made. The four other Board members have each contributed to the changes. Based on their expertise and experience, they have heavily bet on communication and reorganization. The Board's CFO and vice-Chairman have implemented a cost reduction program. A number of unprofitable elements have been rejected. Many changes have taken place at management level, each time motivated by the results that stayed behind.

HR has also kept its end up. The department has organized a range of training courses, targeting all employees and nearly all levels in the organization. These training courses were partially linked to the culture change program—focusing on customer orientation and collaboration.

TILTING

Eighteen months ago, the whole change started with the tilting of the organization. The geographical main division—with a central and relatively autonomous role for the national organizations—was exchanged for a structure with dominant and strategic business lines. Much of the support and staff have been centralized in the process. The purpose was to end the island culture, as well as the island automation.

An ambitious systems, applications and products (SAP) implementation was an important initiative for this project. The Balanced Scorecard was implemented as uniform tool in order to professionalize its management control.

Suppliers were put under pressure to contribute to the improvement of the organization's quality, and in particular the financial performance.

Eighteen months ago, the Chairman of the Board kicked off the process. Meetings were held with all the staff in all the countries; the bad results and the necessity to change and intervene were emphasized during these gatherings. After the presentation of the agenda, drawn up together with an outstanding management consultant, everybody was asked to contribute. After these kick-off meetings followed quarterly pep-talk sessions with the Chairman.

The lack of progress has not gone unnoticed. The works council became increasingly upset. The Supervisory Board supported the launched changes and considered these absolutely necessary. But now, eighteen months later, everyone will want to see results in two weeks' time.

OVERALL PLAN

The meeting with the Supervisory Board and the debate with the works council were both a disaster. The Supervisory Board and the works council both started strongly, not in the least hindered by any self-reflection of their own roles in recent years. The Supervisory Board mainly speaks of the lack of direction and cohesion. Does the Board actually know what they are doing? Are they not out of control? The works council talks of a bad atmosphere in the organization, disorientation, unrest and exhaustion. Excessive change is the cause—according to the works council Chairman anyway.

The evaluation of and the discussions about the changes were not started either during or even after the meeting. A shared reference framework is clearly lacking. What are the actual objectives, besides the necessity to improve on top level and in various project targets and operational measures at lower organization levels? A clear case, comparable with what is required for important investments and take-overs, is missing. There are many plans, but no strategy, no overall plan.

The Board met just after the Christmas holidays. After licking their wounds and establishing that everyone was motivated to keep going, dialogue was started. The focus on action appears to be, as usual, undiminished, especially for the first hour and a half. Had the CFO not slammed the brakes, the next set of plans would already be primed before lunch. The Chairman picked up on the clear signal. "No plans, concrete proposals or final conclusions today," he said.

It was agreed that appreciative assessment and reflection would suffice for now. It was a true dialogue, real attention focused on each other and the situation. At the end of the day, the Chairman summarized the observations, reflections and ideas. The lack of direction and clarity, within the actual team and toward the organization, was a recurring subject.

What else did the Chairman say?
"We want everything, everything is important."

However, making choices and setting priorities seems difficult. "Doing one thing and not letting the other thing go." And: "Let's add that other thing."

Not: "We'll have to pick and choose."

Or: "Let the cobbler stick to his last."

But: "There is no connection any more between want to and can do."

And: "We have asked too much from the organization."

And also: "We have lost touch, we are not getting across to people."

OPENNESS

That day, there was definitely a lot of openness; people took up a vulnerable position. The CFO thinks that he is restricted when it comes to problem-solving, considering the solutions he can apply. "Is that not applicable to the entire team?" the Chairman suggests. "Are we not mainly doing what we are capable of, instead of what is really necessary? Do we actually know what is really necessary? How did we actually start off eighteen months ago?"

Halfway through the afternoon, the question is asked whether the recent period was really all that bad. Project reviews have taken place every second week. These reviews showed that most projects mainly booked positive results; progress and results were rarely behind.

"Many successful operations, yes; but the patient is in a critical condition," replied the Chairman. During dinner he wondered whether they would be able to manage by themselves, considering recent developments and their role. "Can we distance ourselves sufficiently? Will we still have the necessary overview? Do we lack knowledge and experience?"

One of the Board members suddenly remembered the project run by one of the younger managers from Germany, as part of her MBA study. He was interviewed by a psychologist about how the Board was changing the organization. She talked to many people within the organization. The Board member told of how this HR manager spent a lot of time with three senior managers; a country manager and two managers from the strategic business lines. Their interviews had pushed them to ask her for advice.

The Board decides to meet with her, along with one of the three managers, as soon as possible. This meeting takes place just after the New Year. The 36-year-old HR manager, former consultant and university lecturer, is initially honored to be invited. However, she is in the process of accepting a position outside the company. Just after Christmas. the Chairman fills her in on the discussion with the Board members. The HR manager is impressed with the seriousness of the situation, as well as with the open and honest way everything is discussed.

The Board has agreed beforehand to ask the HR manager to adopt a central role in the follow-up of the change process. The discussion goes well, so she is presented with the above-mentioned idea. She reacts enthusiastically, like the senior manager, but she asks for time to reflect.

The parties involved agree to meet up again in three days' time.

STRICT TERMS AND CONDITIONS

This meeting takes place on January 5. Anne, the HR manager's name, is keen to play a central role in the change process. However, she thinks that strict terms and conditions are required in order for her to carry out this mission properly. The Chairman stipulates that position, career perspectives and conditions of employment will not be an issue.

Anne appreciates this but has other conditions in mind and explains her request. As a consultant, she has been confronted before with too little openness and self-reflection from the principal. Based on her first experiences here, that does not seem to be a problem in this situation. However, that is not the case with some other issues.

"During a process of change, especially when initially results don't appear to improve, the reflex of many principals is to say, that things are too abstract or need to be more concrete," explains Anne. "This is not always unjust, but it is often motivated by impatience. Let's agree to speak clearly, but also to get to know each other's professions and utilize instead of disqualify technical language."

Another condition is that Anne's work and that of her team will not be hindered by action reflexes or bad decisiveness. "Think before you act," explains Anne. "Lethal bleeding will of course be stopped, and first aid will be applied if necessary. And I want to be able to choose my own team. 'My' three seniors will be part of that team. As will people with even more knowledge of this business, a couple of transverse thinkers, people with proven experience in complex change processes. And I need people on my team that can combine management and psychological knowledge."

In addition, Anne asks for the necessary authority, including budget and time. The Board has to be principal and sponsor. She must also take the opportunity to involve clients and other stakeholders in the diagnosis and follow-up.

Last but not least, Anne asks if she can 'teach' the Board. The Board will subsequently go and provide what is called 'cascade training' about the *why*, *what* and *how* with regard to the changes. It is then the turn of the department heads to transmit this information to their workers. The Chairman agrees. He cannot resist asking whether Anne has a monopoly on wisdom or comes to preach the gospel.

She listens to him patiently but does not reply directly. Instead, Anne tells the story about Confucius, a famous philosopher from ancient China, well before the foundation of the Chinese empire. One day a student asked Confucius what he would do first if he were asked to rule a country. His answer was: purify the language. The student was surprised until Confucius explained: "If the language is not pure, then the words one speaks are not the same words one means to express. If what you say is not what you mean, things that need to be done will not be dealt with. And then these issues are not resolved, moral and arts deteriorate, justice goes astray and people become confused. And that is the reason why one has to say exactly what one means. This is of the highest importance."

"Point taken," smiles the Chairman, encouragingly.

"The lessons will be planned for next week, two days long," answers Anne.

THE CHANGE COMPETENCE MODEL

The 'lesson' starts with the explanation of pigeonholing and the piecemeal syndrome.

"Complex problems sometimes have simple and logical solutions," says Anne. "But often, that is not the case. Pigeonholing stands for simplifying a complex issue in order to be able to put it in a clear category with the corresponding solution. People don't pick interventions that are suitable, but apply what they know or what has been used successfully in the past."

"Identifiable," says the CFO.

"That's toxic for the proper introduction and implementation of a complex change process," replies Anne. "Now the piecemeal syndrome. That stands for the tendency to handle problems within or in relation to the organization in an isolated manner. This often results in fighting the symptoms. People opt for 'traditional' and 'emotional' reactions, not obstructed by a sharp diagnosis, at the expense of 'rational' reactions: the actions taken after deep and careful consideration of the situation, the objectives, means and effects, including side effects."

"Purposive change is the alternative proposed by American professor Joseph Bower," Anne continues to explain. "This is goal-oriented change that requires and expects determined and efficient behavior."

"Anyway," Anne continues, "the diagnosis is also important with regard to Professor Arjen van Witteloostuijn's 'null hypothesis'."

She explains: "In an ideal situation, the hypothesis for a change initiative should be that change is not necessary. That puts the burden of proof with the people that initiate change. And that automatically requires a solid analysis of the reasons for the change. The costs and the profits, the desirable results and the feasible results, the opportunities and the risks, the pros and the cons; everything has to be made visible and tangible."

"The point is that this approach possibly reinforces or increases the 'us-them,' 'for-against,' 'inside-outside,'" Anne continues. "Many change processes benefit from a common diagnosis. Whether that applies to our situation here will be determined at a later stage. Anyhow, the analysis mentioned is the basis for the business case in relation to the change: the *change case*. And that is often lacking. A business case is drawn up for any important investment or purchase, whereas this is omitted for drastic changes within the organization, even though the entire organization might be turned upside down on organizational and emotional level. To have a view on the literal and figurative costs and profits is essential for the success of a change initiative."

Before she started her course, Anne was a bit tense, but now she sees that she has captivated her audience.

"Now, Confucius, the common language, saying, meaning, doing," she continues confidently. "Change is a continuous and dynamic process. Professional change causes planning and learning, structure and improvisation, intentional and spontaneous changes to go hand-in-hand."

Anne draws two 'eights' on the white Board, one vertical, one horizontal. They come together in the middle where she draws a round shape. Around the total figure she draws a circle, unsteady but flowing with a gap left and right.

"This 'circle'," she says, "is the context within which the organization and the change have to 'function.' Partially predictable, partially unpredictable. Often identifiable, sometimes unrecognizable. The context requires, dictates, challenges, restricts, offers opportunities, forces, invites, activates, motivates, cradles, embraces you, surprises or kills. Correct functioning, efficient change requires a good connection between context, strategy, change and organization. Between wishing and being able to, desirable and feasible, objective and means. The vertical 'eight' stands for the objective, the vision of change," explains Anne. "The horizontal 'eight' signifies the means, the feasibility or the capacity to change. Together they constitute The Change Competence Model."

"That is a beautiful and inspirational drawing," the CFO comments. "Lemniscate, infinite sign, Oriental, a church window. But what do those five zones mean?"

"Thank you for the introductory contemplations," replies Anne. "It is all you mentioned. But first your 'zones.'"

And she starts to explain, passionately. "The top zone stands for the Rationale and the bottom for the Effect of the change. If those two are connected and clear, then you will have a change vision. The Rationale signifies the motivation, the *why* of the change. The Rationale will have to correspond with strategic logics or a corporate story; but above all it has to appeal, touch people. Logically and visionary, cognitive and affective. The bottom zone Effect represents the costs and revenues, the advantages and disadvantages, positive and negative results and perceptions and feelings regarding the change of those involved."

"The 'eight' can also be found in Oriental martial arts," tells Anne. "Head, heart and belly. When they are in line and connected, everything else also functions. The left vertical zone stands for Focus, the right one for Energy. When they are connected they form the change capacity, the means to realize the objective, the feasible. Focus controls behavior and describes and stimulates the direction of the change. Focus is about prevailing circumstances like organization values, strategy, structure, reward programs and example behavior that shape behavior and choices. Energy signifies the fuel for change: inspiration, motivation and ability. But also budget, time, creativity, knowledge and experience about change."

CONNECTION

The Board members are listening attentively.

"Connection is another story," Anne continues. "The function is connecting the other four factors or zones and the two 'eights'. But Connection also means control, guidance and solidarity, consistency and cohesion. In a way, without Connection the other zones and the corresponding efforts and results are useless. Piecemeal syndrome, fighting symptoms. Therefore, Connection is also called the heart of change. The four other zones make up the blood circulation of the change."

Anne presents another comparison: "This is maybe a productive metaphor for you. Beating heart. Blood pressure. Heart attack. Bypasses. Cholesterol. Silent Killers. Life. Love with all your heart."

The CFO immediately adds: "With heart and soul. Open-heart operation. Heart drugs. Clogged arteries. Healthy lifestyle. Arteriosclerosis. Athlete's heart."

Anne smiles. "A great completion of this first long day. We'll continue tomorrow with dysfunctions, strategies and interventions. Be prepared! And remember, we are learning a language. Don't ask me to be more concrete. Considering your responsibilities and ambitions, you can't afford intellectual poverty or laziness. Moreover, we will also discuss leadership roles tomorrow. I will try and test you. I'll tell you about the Storyteller, the Architect, the Framer, the Resource Allocator, the Shepherd, the Controller and a couple of other figures. You have been warned."

After dinner, the CFO once more brings up his reaction about the 'eights.' He tells Anne and his colleagues how intrigued he is by the visualization and the striking dynamics. The cohesion between the factors and the role of Connection is even more fascinating, he says.

In the bar, Anne reacts by telling a story about Aalt, a teacher and martial artist, with whom she collaborated regularly during her time as a teacher and consultant.

His slogan: 'Lacking one, is none.' "The essence of what managers and consultants try to express with definitions such as integrality and agreement," explains Anne.

When she shared the 'two eights pattern' with him, Aalt saw the infinite sign in the horizontal eight, change as a continuous, constant process. But most of all he reacted on the vertical 'eight' and the center of the connecting zone.

According to Anne, Aalt mainly saw this as head, heart and belly. Change is only possible when these three elements are 'one,' in line with each other, connected. Thinking and acting have to be connected with and by the heart.

Robbert, the fourth member of the Board, has been listening attentively and in silence to Anne's story. He worked with Aalt for years. What he remembers most were the words 'awake' and 'breath.' Robbert explains: "According to Aalt, it is all about breath because without breath there is no life."

"That connects nicely to the comparison of the heart from this afternoon," the Chairman comments. "Indeed," reacts Anne.

And Robbert continues: "A breathing organization is an organization that's awake. An organization that 'sees' and 'feels', often also 'knows' what's going on, inside and outside the organization."

"Maybe we should continue on this path tomorrow morning," Anne proposes.

MULTIPLE PERSPECTIVES

The next day, Anne unexpectedly starts with a photograph of the disaster with the *Herald of Free Enterprise*. This ferry capsized on March 6, 1987, near Zeebrugge, Belgium, and nearly two hundred people lost their lives. Many people think that the cause is as serious as it is simple: a loading bridge that was not properly closed. "That is a reassuring explanation," says Anne: "Loading bridge properly closed equals no disaster."

"Research carried out by psychologist Prof. Dr. Willem Albert Wagenaar shows that many, extremely varied factors, large and small, technical and human, internal and external, together caused the disaster. That is a lesson to be learned. In any case that you have to be prepared and able to apply several lenses, paradigms, perspectives or disciplines and corresponding concepts in order to obtain a picture of the situation that is as complete and adequate as possible."

"Therefore," Anne continues, "I will present you today with additional perspectives and concepts, based on our five factors or zones and Context as a sixth one. Those perspectives relate to dysfunctions, leadership and change approaches. These additional elements provide you with the option to perceive and act in a varied or multiple ways. Yesterday's factors and the 'two eights pattern' guarantee cohesion and integrality. Consider that pattern as a map. It can be used during your voyage or process to determine where you are, where you want to go and how the zones are related and connected!"

DYSFUNCTIONS

Anne announces that she is now going to talk about the organizational dysfunctions associated with the Change Competence Model.

"When you have to deal with dysfunctions, you are busy finding out why the change is not working or what you need to solve before you can carry through change. Dysfunctions can occur when a factor such as the Rationale is not (sufficiently) present or when the factor is incorrectly completed. If a proper completion of Effect is lacking, people can't see the personal advantage of change—the yield. Or they don't feel obligated to contribute— the obligation. If the Effect has been wrongly completed, then the high costs of change—for example, having to relocate—are characteristic obstacles. Or incorrect information results in employees' wrong, negative estimation of the consequences of the change."

The lesson continues with the statement that besides singular dysfunctions, there are also multiple ones. "That is the case when two or more factors or zones form the problem," says Anne. "When the Rationale and the Focus are detached from the rest, there is question of the 'Ivory Tower.' The top has been separated from the rest of the organization. Visions and plans are centrally formulated and implemented in a directive way, without a vision on or feeling for what is happening in the rest of the organization. When Energy and Effect are detached from the whole, the dysfunction Egoism occurs. The result is that professionals do not take a common vision or policy into consideration and do their own thing, alone or as a group. There is no cohesion or connection and only own, often individual, performances and professional standards give satisfaction and motivate."

"And then we still have integral dysfunctions," Anne continues. "That is a situation on fire or very inflammable. Sometimes it is a peat-moor fire, sometimes a raging fire. In any case, the consequences are disastrous and huge if nothing is done."

Anne gives another example of an organization where she worked as a consultant three years ago, a 'disintegrated organization' as the project manager put it at the time. She describes a large health care organization where the decentralized units each made their own plan. Top management was not capable of controlling the situation through positive reinforcing mechanisms or corrective mechanisms. There was question of emotional detachment. Organization elements and individuals went 'below the surface' and withdrew. The corporate citizenship was completely undermined. A 'civil war' was raging: groups and their opinions fought with each other, or each determined their territory. Collaboration was lacking, there was little attention for the environment outside the organization and survival of the fittest was the adage.

"In short, a very serious situation," says Anne, "but luckily not applicable to the situation here."

"That just shows, it can always be worse somewhere else," jokes the Chairman.

"Is that true?" asks Dave, one of the Board members. "Anne, I understand that you and your team still want to carry out an extensive diagnosis. But with all possible reservations, what is our dysfunction?"

Anne looks up a sheet with the integral dysfunctions, clearly summed up and described. "I'm just going to do something else. Study this sheet and reflect on your own situation. We'll discuss your verdict half an hour before lunch."

DISRUPTIVE

The Board reports one hour later. They have some reservations, mumble something about 'educated guesses' and 'best guesses' and then start. Dave, the member who asked "Is that true?" reports.

It appears that, in principle, everybody agrees about the dysfunction. However, there is disagreement about the answer on the question whether the dysfunction is less serious than in the health care organization that Anne has described in her example. In any case, the dysfunction was as integral and disturbing, but with a completely different content and presented in a different form.

Listing and describing the dysfunctions has been effective for the Board team, Anne observes. The team comes up with the integral dysfunction Disruptive when considering their own change process. Some elements in the description, such as the tough battle between the old coalition and the reformers, past and present, were not really under discussion. But most elements were discussed. Because: Different realities, for a start within the Board, are in conflict. Control and change do not ensure a good combination of flexibility and stability, but obstruct each other.

Allocation of means and establishing priorities have become an unsteady process, Anne thinks. Initiatives and projects trip over each other. Daily quotations! One day it's this, the next day something else. Managers and employees are disorientated. Priorities are not clear. "Organizational confusion," emphasizes Anne. "Priority proliferation, everything and therefore nothing is important."

The CFO adds that elements of disorganization have also been recognized in the observation. It was mostly about the lack of vision and direction and the missing compelling story.

A joint evaluation reveals that the content-related result and this first interpretation of the integral dysfunction are valuable. According to the team, the true profit is in focused and conscious thinking about the change process within your own organization. Systematic searching, stock-taking, confronting and assessing while speaking the same language.

Anne endorses this and indicates that the result of this exercise can form a perfect base for a next step: considering leadership roles and learning which styles, competences and combinations are conditional or essential in different phases and situations.

During lunch, the team exchanges thoughts about their own and each other's leadership style. A year ago, the team did an assessment. The insights and language learned during that assessment have given some direction to the discussion but at the time they got stuck on the question what change really requires, what functions will have to be fulfilled.

LEADERSHIP

After lunch, Anne explains which leadership roles are important in the event of change. She describes how the Rationale requires a Strategist, someone who is capable of formulating strategic logics, a content-related vision or a business model.

She also specifies that this is not all, far from it. "The content has to agree but also appeal," Anne explains. "Besides the Strategist, the role of the Storyteller is essential. The Rationale is not the reason but the motivation. It is about the cognitive side, but also about the emotional side, the instinctive element."

After having explained and illustrated the twelve roles, including the Visionary and Boundary Spanner linked to the Context zone, Anne explains the connection with dysfunctions as discussed this morning. "Say, there is question of the Ivory Tower whereby Rationale and Focus have been detached from the rest. Where did it go wrong? Or are the leadership and the roles to be blamed?"

Anne does not wait for the team to reply and comes up with the answer herself.

"In that case, top management is probably with its head in the clouds. The Visionary, Strategist and Architect are building well-designed castles in the sky. Changes are mostly initiated top-down. They are not connected to employees and other stakeholder movements, feelings and motivations. The Shepherd and the Resource Allocator have been put out of action, or are insufficiently used. The Controller and Translator can't or won't do their work."

Anne gives a second example, the dysfunction Egoism, also discussed this morning. In this organization, Energy and Effect have been detached from the rest of the organization. Professionals, teams, units are doing their own thing. They have their own standards, invest in their personal or hand-picked objectives, but not in the organization. The Rationale is not fulfilled, or does not function. The Strategist and Storyteller cannot formulate and transmit a collective ambition. Managers are 'out of balance,' teamed with their employees but disconnected from the organization as a whole. Focus and Effect are not effective for the entire organization; the Architect, Framer and Controller do not discipline and correct.

Then it is time to put the self-assessment of the own organization into practice by means of leadership roles. The basic assumption is the dysfunction Disruptive—suggested by the Board team as a possible explanation for the situation in which their own organization now finds itself. Anne proposes to present an 'overview from the textbook' as basis for the discussion about recognizability, correctness and possible signification for the current situation. She stresses that leadership roles have to be filled correctly in accordance with the specific phase or context. Only then can the question about who in a team or organization fills in the role be dealt with.

Anne describes the chosen dysfunction at a high pace and building on yesterday's 'lessons' and exchange of thoughts. "Because different leadership roles, especially the Integrator, Storyteller, Controller and Framer, *don't* function, there are different realities and visions within the organization. They are in conflict. The bearing forces from the past and the present are often in competition with reformers and new blood. The Visionary, Strategist and Integrator are at loggerheads with the Architect, Controller and Resource Allocator. The necessary control and desired changes are not in proportion with each other. Managers and employees are in the dark as too many instructions are given. However, priorities are not structured. Everything is important and therefore nothing matters anymore."

"That sounds like fun," says Rebecca cynically, who joined the Board last year. "Where do we start in such a situation?"

"What do we start with?" questions the action-oriented CFO.

"That's going to be difficult," replies Robbert cynically.

Rebecca: "It's an example, but also very applicable to our situation. In any case, we have to use the example, considering the huge task in front of us. Let's start!"

The Chairman doesn't say a word.

Anne waits. And then she suddenly exclaims: "We have started already!" She looks each Board team member in the eye. "You have made a decision already. That's why we are spending these two days together. Those days are nearly over. We now have a common language and reference framework. There is work to be done: common diagnosis, null hypothesis, change case, leadership roles. The approaches to change are not dealt with now, that can be done later when we establish our plan." Anne continues: "We must first involve and manage our people to get them on board, is this not the highest priority?"

Robbert hesitates. "I understand what you're saying but I think that HR is going to say they will solve this in the coming month, at the very least with regard to the soft side."

"What do you mean?" asks Anne.

"Well, we have a complete set of leadership trips planned, haven't we?" answers Robbert. "Entire groups of managers and employees are going to work on their personal leadership and connection. Talking about involvement and reaching people . . ."

"Yes, and during the year the outside will be shaped with the help of the employees by means of the next step in the Balanced Scorecard implementation," adds the CFO. "After the first set of performance indicators has been determined top-down, we are now going to work bottom-up with countries, departments, business lines and individual employees!"

"Stop," Rebecca shouts. "Stop, there we go again. Piecemeal syndrome, pigeonholing! Do you remember?"

The Chairman contemplates this and says: "What should we do?"

Anne: "It is now Friday 7 p.m. Time for some rest, relaxation and self-reflection. Catch your breath and have a good sleep so that the team is 'awake' next week." She hands everyone a parcel. "Enjoy the read!"

The Chairman thanks everybody. "We'll continue Monday morning."

That evening, the Chairman is content when he looks back on these two days. They have not spared each other. Without a doubt this has been one of the most intensive and demanding meetings he has ever attended. However, he does not feel tired.

He looks at the parcel. In beautiful tricolor wrapping paper. He unwraps the parcel and looks at the book cover: *Change Competence: Implementing Effective Change.* He opens the book and starts reading . . .

8 The Change Case—Part II

MONDAY MORNING

After the weekend, during which the Chairman read the book, he asked Anne: "What now, what do you need?"

"The key to the cabinet with the five million first, and then three days on the *Change Competence Canvas*" was the reply.

"What cabinet? And what's the Change Competence Canvas?" asked the Chairman.

"I'll start with the canvas," replied Anne, "because I can be brief about that one for now. The Change Competence Canvas is an interactive working method that is tied to the Change Competence Model. It enables you to make several diagnoses with a group, in order to see and experience which problems and dysfunctions are present within the organization. But it also enables you to observe, for example, which leadership roles are present and which are missing in order to realize change successfully. It generates essential insights for the formulation of proper change goals and the design of a change strategy that is congruent with the possibilities of the organization. But more on that later."

"The cabinet with the five million, then. It, literally and figuratively, contains the insights, lessons, analyses, advise, reports and evaluations that have been produced in recent years in order to move this organization forward. This organization doesn't realize what knowledge it already possesses. Much has already been researched, analyzed and learned. But there is also a lot that has not been used, or has simply been forgotten. That is not only a serious waste of energy, knowledge, experience and opportunities, but also a source of frustration for many people within this organization. And if we open this cabinet, we hit two birds with one stone. And more. We acknowledge the work that has already been done, and we value the people who were involved in these projects. With a limited additional investment, we increase our knowledge and perceptions for the diagnosis. The change history and the basis for future activities are brought into the picture. We prevent things from being done over and over again. We can learn from the past, from things that did or didn't happen."

"Great idea, but don't forget, we are talking about a rich collection and each element has its own history," said the Chairman. "Maybe this 'cabinet' contains a total investment that is much larger than the amount you mention. In any case, it contains a multiple of that amount in frustration, resistance and other irritations."

"But undoubtedly also many useful or even beautiful tools that deserve a second chance. The return could be huge in terms of improvement, ideas, motivation, new perspectives, drive and energy," said Anne. "Moreover, not only does it concern elements and results that are not fully used on an individual level, but it is also about the lack of cohesion and evaluation of all those alternatives and projects based on a clear direction, a common framework."

"Yes," said the Chairman, "now that you mention it, are we not lacking that direction and framework?"

"I think you are," said Anne. "The motive and the direction were missing. Therefore we are now confronted with initiative after initiative, without prioritization and without cohesion. Anything goes."

"So . . . ," said the Chairman.

"So, the motive and direction, Rationale and Focus, have to be provided," said Anne.

"Who should be involved in that process?" asked the Chairman.

"It depends," said Anne, "what is the level of involvement, what is our assessment of the professionalism and psychological maturity of our people?"

"Do you know?" asked the Chairman.

"No," said Anne, "I have a feeling and a vision, but we have to carry out a thorough assessment. We can do this by measuring and finding out what the capacity for change currently is, and the dysfunctions and the opportunities. We have a method with practical questionnaires for that. But it is also about the further development of the feeling and the vision by starting a discussion, seeing people and presenting yourself as management. By doing this, you'll find out what's happening on the work floor and then things will start moving. Take it from me; as long as you don't make contact and don't connect in this specific situation, any approach or intervention is wasted energy. It is about relatedness as a basis for the further process of change."

"Ok," said the Chairman, "but those three days and that canvas, that sounds like boot camp."

"It is kind of a boot camp, although I won't be your instructor or trainer, like I was for those two days last week, but I can be your guide and explorer. In the coming weeks, we'll work on the measuring, we empty that 'cabinet' and restore contact with the organization, then three days with the Board and your top 30."

"What is the program?" asked the Chairman.

"That depends on our experiences in the coming weeks, but I can tell you the objective and the function. We'll establish the *change case*. We will realize a common diagnosis, define the change goals, learn to prioritize and assess, look at the leadership roles and draft a change process with strategy and approaches. Before this, the top 30 will get two days as you have had. Clarity, language, Confucius, cascade. You are co-trainers."

"One thing," said the Chairman: "Draft sounds like 'little.'"

"One of my masters is Sennett," said Anne. "He writes about 'the craftsman' and the importance of the 'draft'.[1] The craftsman is skilled but at the beginning of the process doesn't know exactly what he is going to do. A good craftsman starts with an open mind but not a blank mind. He starts the process with the best professional knowledge and experience and the best tools available, but does not take this as an absolute element or idealize it and commences 'a discussion' with the specific context. Sennett relates this to the advice to set up a structure that does justice to the available knowledge and perceptions but that can develop in relation to the dynamic context. That is our draft. Not a little, not everything, but quite a lot.

"Now, the Change Competence Canvas in more detail. The Change Competence Canvas represents the literal, figurative, content-related and symbolic basis for the change process. Canvas is a strong, solid fabric. It is also the base for a painting. Not more, not less. Our base is such a fabric onto which the (for you, now well-known) Change Competence Model with its two 'eights' and definitions, such as Rationale and Energy, are projected. During the three days, we create our draft on these elements. The 'painting' will develop itself during the change process that follows. Over the three days, we will work in an interactive and dynamic way on the Change Competence Canvas of 30 by 30 feet with the group. We assess, discuss, work on a dialogue, design and develop, chose our position, compare, acquire insight into leadership roles."

"That does appeal to me," said the Chairman, "although, of course, I don't understand all of it yet, but I rely on your craftsmanship and your sketchbook."

However, something still seemed to bother the Chairman. Anne asked him what it was. "Anne, you have confronted me and the team with the consequences of excessive change. You have made us see that we resided in our 'ivory tower' at crucial moments. How can we avoid making the same mistake again? I'm worried about our managers and employees. What do we have to do to restore the contact? What is a priority besides relatedness?"

"My advice, my assessment?" Anne asked. "I think there is a need for clarity and fair process, self-efficacy and action control, a balance between freedom and security."

"That's quite a lot," said the Chairman, "you mean a good balance between control and self-control, autonomy and control?"

"The last thing I want is to speak in riddles. Can I explain?" Anne asked.

The Chairman laughed apologetically and nodded.

"It is important that people know again what they have to do and what is expected from them. They have to be able to deliver useful contributions and see their position and function within the context of the larger entity. The necessary clarity requires direction from management. Sociologist Zygmunt Bauman is my inspiration for this. It is about the balance or good relationship between freedom and security.[2] Especially if our first conclusion from the two-day session is correct, that here we are dealing with a Disruptive dysfunction. Bauman states that security without freedom is bondage or slavery. Freedom without security is chaos, insecurity and powerlessness. A fair process is very important, as the coming period will require choices that will not be profitable for everybody. Consequently, it is of great importance to ensure procedural justice. And that means a clear, fair and interactive process. Any possible negative effects resulting from change for groups or individuals are easier to digest and to accept when a fair process is used."

"I understand that, but we are in a hurry, something has to happen quickly," the Chairman said.

"I forgot about that. Besides the key, the three days and the trust you have just given me, I will also need time," Anne added.

"How much?" asked the Chairman.

"More than you are used to take as a manager," replied Anne.

"What do you mean?"

Anne replied with a short story.

"If you add 100,000 joule to an egg in five minutes by heating it, you get a boiled egg. But if your aim was to hatch a chick you would need 1,000 times more energy and 6,000 times more time—next to a chicken or an incubator, of course. The time pressure that many managers experience creates a situation in which they would like to produce a chick within five minutes, tops."

The Chairman gave Anne the green light and she started immediately.

The cabinet is opened. With a team of ten people, hand-picked, Anne maps out the change history, all projects, findings, analyses and advise. Every element gets a first assessment. What is the quality, to what extent is it used, what is the potential, in which situations can it be applied, why has it worked or not worked, what must happen for it to work, what other elements does it relate to, what dependencies are there? Then they looked for patterns. In a process of consensual validation, the team obtains a number of important insights. Anne is satisfied. *Food for thought*. A good start to the three-day session.

THE TWO TRAINING DAYS

The 'analysis of the cabinet' took almost four weeks. One week later the training course for the top 30 was on the program, as preparation for the three-day session that would follow some time later. Anne was in charge of the training days; the members of the Board were co-trainers. After the introduction and a presentation of the program, the Chairman began to speak.

"An old man who was on his deathbed called his sons in order to give them a last piece of advice and to say farewell. He asked his servants to bring him a bundle of branches and said to his oldest son: 'Break the bundle in two!' The son tried his utmost but did not manage to break the bundle. The other sons tried as well but none of them succeeded. Then the father said: 'Untie the bundle and take one branch each.' When they had done that he said: 'Break the branch in two!' and the branch broke easily. 'Now you see what I mean,' said the father."

Everyone was silent.

The Chairman continued: "From the best intentions, but with too little awareness, I have asked you time after time to break that bundle of branches alone. Many times I have tried it myself too, as have my colleagues on the Board. What Anne calls excessive change is the result of the unruly initiatives to change *and* the way we have managed and collaborated. I would like to apologize. The beautiful story from Aesop, about the breaking of a bundle of branches, shows that an alternative exists."

The CFO stood up. He said: "My sister Iris is a professor in developmental psychology. Her 'hero' is Wilfried Bion, a British psychiatrist and expert in the field of group dynamics. Iris had her oration two weeks ago and Bion's approach played an important role in her speech." The CFO took a piece of paper from his pocket and read: "When Bion visited New York, he wanted to see the Picasso's anti-war painting 'Guernica.' When Bion saw the painting he was overcome by emotion. The painting evoked strong memories. Bion told that he had served in WWI as a tank officer. He had noticed that soldiers who had been exposed to fire, sound and violence suffered from shell shock. He himself and his team had the protection of a tank. It served as a container, offering safety and shelter, physically as well as mentally. This is analogous to a child in the first years of its life. That child needs a parent in order to deal with fear, pain and confusion that are often accompany the confrontation with new surroundings and stages of development. To the young child, the love, warmth and protection of the parent is the container."[3] He continued: "Iris also talked about the attachment theory of the British psychiatrist Bowlby. I have learned that leaders, similar to the parent-child relation, have to provide a safe attachment for their people. Leaders then form the operational base for the exploration of the new environment, in situations of stress, insecurity and change. Safe attachment, as Iris explained to me, requires leaders with a sensitive attitude, who respect the followers' autonomy and support and structure the followers' learning and change process. That is possibly in complete contrast to my own style and skills. But fortunately, not everything depends on me and I have decided to do everything in my capacity to provide a contribution."

Anne reacts: "We are going to talk about the question how we can transform excessive change into productive change. In order to do so, we have to master and speak the same language. Confucius teaches us that only then we can clarify what we mean and can understand what is meant."

She explains the Change Competence Canvas and illustrates definitions such as Rationale and Energy. Then she explains how the organization gets from Context to change goals and how you can convert these into a change strategy, approaches and concrete interventions.

One of the most experienced people in the top 30 reacts: "That sounds quite exemplary. Like a blueprint. As if there is a recipe for the difficult situation we are in."

"Eric, did you miss out on the story about the psychiatrists and the process structures?" says a colleague.

"Not to mention containment!" replies Eric laughing.

For the first time that morning, Anne projects a sheet. A dated black-and-white photograph of a southern European man with messy hair appeared. "This is Spyros Makridakis, professor at Insead. He also uses, not by coincidence, the analogy of the recipe. Makridakis says that cookbooks make the same recipes available to everybody. But despite this, there are very few great chefs. He quotes one of the great chefs, Roger Verge." Anne shows a picture of Verge and his quote on the right:

> *"A recipe is not meant to be followed exactly—it's a canvas on which you can embroider. Add a zest to this, a drop or two of that, a tiny pinch of the other. Let yourself be led by your palate and your tongue, your eyes and your heart. In other words, be guided by your love of food, and then you will be able to cook."*

"Who is the chef?" cries Karen, one of the great talents in the management group. The reference to the well-known Dutch cooking show doesn't escape most of them and they laugh and comment loudly.

"You, all of us, everybody," Anne says.

"Isn't that easy?" another manager asks.

"No," says Alain, a fourth member of the Board. "Last year I was able to spend a number of weeks at Harvard. I attended a lecture by Ronald Heifetz. He taught me a lot and opened my eyes. Heifetz says that it is probably more useful to define leadership as an *activity* instead of a hierarchic position, a set of competences in a social structure or a set of personality characteristics. When you consider it an *activity,* leadership can be provided from various positions in the organization. High, low, line, employees, everyone can accept his/her role. Everybody's qualities are better used, overloading a couple of 'high-ranking employees' is avoided and you can react faster and more efficiently to specific situations!"

The Chairman adds: "During our two-day session, Anne showed us a whole collection of leadership roles so extensive and varied, that a summing up alone would make it clear that all these roles can never be filled in by a small team, let alone by one person. The roles often have a very different content and some are in conflict with each other. We need each other and everyone's specific qualities. Together we need to learn to create the right combinations and link roles and individual qualities to the numerous and varied questions that we will encounter in the time to come!"

Dave, one of the country managers, asks: "Are we not making this too complex? Is it not simply a question of writing a proper plan and following that plan?!"

Anne reacts: "Thanks, Dave. Alain has just talked about Heifetz and Harvard. Heifetz distinguishes between technical and adaptive changes or challenges. The first type can be dealt with by applying existing technical knowledge, techniques and routine behavior. It is about 'treating the illness.' Expertise and good management are enough. In the event of adaptive changes, the 'illness' is a condition, but not the actual problem. The danger is that we will try and solve a non-technical problem with a technical solution."

"And that is a huge mistake," Eric says.

"In any way, it doesn't help," says Anne, "and that is possibly what we have experienced ourselves in recent years with the numerous change initiatives." She continues: "The patient has to face some essential questions in the event of adaptive change, like 'What do I do with the rest of my life?' and 'How do I make sure that my family is looked after?' With these types of questions, there is tension or a gap between your own values and the concrete circumstances that confront you. Leadership is supposed to bridge the gap. Leaders are guides, or even liberators or re-creators. They bring the organization to a next phase and allow transformation. They have to ensure a supply of energy, time, money, means and 'finds' in order to influence circumstances in a positive way."

"In our situation, we are probably dealing with a combination of technical and adaptive problems, aren't we?" Dave asks.

"I don't exclude that," says Anne. "The trick is to rise above the dust and see the patterns or syndromes that are present. Heifetz calls that 'getting on the balcony.' The three days that will follow allow you to do just that!"

The top 30 and the five Board members spent the remainder of the two days mainly on the canvas. Sometimes Anne taught, but more often they talked to each other in the new common language.

THE DIAGNOSIS

The three-day session starts. Thanks to Dave and Karen's initiative, there are 65 participants instead of 35. A second group of 30 is formed in addition to the initial group of 30 plus the 5 members of the Board. A second group which can be consulted during the process, provides reflection and can be used to test the results. This group works on certain elements parallel to the top 30. Anne's team ensures facilitation and coordination. The entire group starts off in a large room, standing around the 30 by 30 feet canvas. The Chairman stands in the middle of the canvas and starts talking. On the wall behind him is a painting by John Gilbert, of the battle of Agincourt between the English and the French in 1415. The Chairman is a history buff and particularly interested in the military and literary art of painting.

"During the battle of Agincourt, on 25 October 1415, St Crispin's Day, the English army defeated the French army even though they were far out-numbered. Rumors say that the ratio was 1 to 6. The English were fighting on French territory under the command of Henry V. The battle played a role in Shakespeare's *Henry V* (1599), in which the tensions a king has to deal with play an important part. A king is supposed to be royal, fair and just. At the same time, he must be capable of ruthlessness and 'Machiavellian-ism.' Before the battle commences, Henry V speaks to his troops. The heroic *Saint Crispin's Day Speech* oozes honor, military glory, love of country and self-sacrifice."[4]

WESTMORELAND.

O that we now had here.
But one ten thousand of those men in England.
That do no work today!

KING HENRY V.

What's he that wishes so?
My cousin Westmoreland? No, my fair cousin:
If we are mark'd to die, we are enow
To do our country loss; and if to live,
The fewer men, the greater share of honour.
God's will! I pray thee, wish not one man more.
By Jove, I am not covetous for gold,
Nor care I who doth feed upon my cost;
It yearns me not if men my garments wear;
Such outward things dwell not in my desires:
But if it be a sin to covet honour,
I am the most offending soul alive.
No, faith, my coz, wish not a man from England:
God's peace! I would not lose so great an honour
As one man more, methinks, would share from me
For the best hope I have. O, do not wish one more!
Rather proclaim it, Westmoreland, through my host,
That he which hath no stomach to this fight,
Let him depart; his passport shall be made
And crowns for convoy put into his purse:
We would not die in that man's company
That fears his fellowship to die with us.
This day is called the feast of Crispian:
He that outlives this day, and comes safe home,
Will stand a tip-toe when the day is named,

And rouse him at the name of Crispian.
He that shall live this day, and see old age,
Will yearly on the vigil feast his neighbours,
And say 'To-morrow is Saint Crispian:'
Then will he strip his sleeve and show his scars.
And say 'These wounds I had on Crispin's day.'
Old men forget: yet all shall be forgot,
But he'll remember with advantages
What feats he did that day: then shall our names.
Familiar in his mouth as household words
Harry the king, Bedford and Exeter,
Warwick and Talbot, Salisbury and Gloucester,
Be in their flowing cups freshly remember'd.
This story shall the good man teach his son;
And Crispin Crispian shall ne'er go by,
From this day to the ending of the world,
But we in it shall be remember'd;
We few, we happy few, we band of brothers;
For he to-day that sheds his blood with me
Shall be my brother; be he ne'er so vile,
This day shall gentle his condition:
And gentlemen in England now a-bed
Shall think themselves accursed they were not here,
And hold their manhoods cheap whiles any speaks
That fought with us upon Saint Crispin's day.

"Shakespeare's description is one of the first examples in English literature in which solidarity and comradeship were linked to victory in battle. For me this is a good reason to tell you this story, but not the most important one. Despite their great number, the French were routed. A number of factors played a role, individually or jointly. Henry's counterpart, Charles VI, did not command the French army himself as he struggled with illness and mental problems. The French were convinced that their huge army and superior cavalry, with about 1,200 knights on horseback, were invincible. They were over-confident and arrogant. The circumstances at the location were muddy and unfavorable for the 'heavy' French cavalry. Etcetera, etcetera."

The Chairman stopped talking for a moment.

"What I want to discuss with you is motivation and a reason to fight. Our organization is suffering from the numerous impulses of 'want to' and 'have to.' Excessive change. We move, we are energetic but we are also running around like headless chickens. 'Much ado about nothing.' Direction was missing, a lack of Focus. That concerns me personally. We are too focused on ourselves and are missing out on what is going on around us. In the past few weeks, we have realized a first diagnosis, and we have studied the internal and external context. And if we are not careful, we will be run over. In the past year, two of our competitors have developed at an alarming pace. It shows in everything: their market share, the financial results, analysts' judgment, clients that switch company, etc. As well as the determining factors mentioned for the Agincourt battle, the 'picture of the enemy' was very important. That is the real reason why I am telling you this story. At this moment in particular, we cannot and may no longer ignore that our enemies are stronger than ever and we are more vulnerable than before. The French were obsessed with their cavalry. History also shows that the English archers played a decisive role. The opinions about the next part of the story differ. But as a parable, it is a gem."

To the surprise of a number of the people present, the Chairman sticks up his index and middle finger, 'two fingers up.' He looks around and continues with his story.

"The story goes that the French threatened to chop off these two fingers of every English archer they captured. Talk about Effect. The two most important fingers for an archer. The threat could have had far-reaching practical consequences, but in any case acquired a clear symbolic meaning. The archers knew what they had to do. The rest is history. The story goes that after the victory, the archers triumphantly and provocatively stuck up the two fingers to whatever French soldiers that had survived. The V of Victory is the positive version, according to some."

Anne presents the internal and external analysis. The 'five million cabinet' is doing its job. Respect, appreciation and acknowledgement live among those present. But there is also a lot of unrest, dismay and surprise. 'All that work and so little result'; 'the left hand doesn't even know what the right hand is doing'; 'such potential, great to have an overview now'; 'why didn't we do this before?'; ' what a waste of energy, manpower and money'; 'many good things but I can't do anything with it'. 'who thought of all of this?'; 'great find!'; 'is the situation really that bad'; 'it's incomprehensible that we have missed that movement?!'; 'they are much further than I thought'; and 'we have underestimated the situation' were expressions that were heard.

Anne reacts: "You emphasize the necessity to act. But if we don't do this based on a common and thoroughly considered diagnosis and a collective ambition, all effort will be in vain. The only difference is that then, we are driven by bitter necessity and aimless ambition. Disorder will rapidly be succeeded by blind panic."

The Chairman resumes: "Let's stay in the military atmosphere: An army is at its most vulnerable when the marching is transformed into order of battle. Right now we are more vulnerable than we have ever been. We have to close the ranks."

Under Anne's supervision, and flanked by the 5 Board members in their capacity as co-trainers, a group diagnosis was made on the Change Competence Canvas, based on two questions: What are we good at in this organization when it comes to change, and what has priority when it comes to improvement? Everybody answered both questions, the Board and the top 30, by picking a place on the canvas. For the first question, the Rationale and Focus were overpopulated. Connection was a popular choice for question two, with the Effect a good second. Rationale and Focus were also relatively 'well' populated. Anne crisscrossed over the canvas and asked for explanations. "Why are you on the Rationale? Why do you choose Energy? What does Connection mean for you? Does it surprise you that so many people qualified Rationale and Focus as 'good'?" Anne managed to evoke an important leadership element: humble inquiry.

Motivated by the work of Anne's team, the common diagnosis is decided upon with much energy. The dysfunctions Disruptive, Selfishness, Disorientation and the Ivory Tower fight for priority. Dialogue and reflection, in combination with the humble inquiry, do the rest. The 'change draft' is taking shape. The contact and the connection within this group are beginning to restore; a great start. The Top 30 decides to model the cascade further, in conjunction with the Board. There will be comparable sessions on the subsequent levels, toward the units and teams, with clear frameworks, non-negotiable minimum behavior and room for testing, development and fine tuning every time. There will be a synthesis between 'bottom-up' and 'top-down.' The CFO calls this 'phase 0.'

And the end of the second day and before starting the third day, the top 30 and the 30 other guests get stuck on the question of how the change should be approached. They agree that contact must be restored. The cascade is the means to do so. Heifetz's statement, that leadership mainly implies activities rather than positions, is an important starting point. Managers reflect on that starting point by means of Bion's and Bowlby's theories. Definitions like 'survival,' 'concerned leadership' and 'quiet leadership' can be heard. Giving direction and using that as a base to work in a consistent and coherent way is another shared opinion.

The top 30 argues for an approach focused on inspiration of the troops. For them, direction is mainly the development of a collective ambition, the corporate story, and a common reference point. The 'other' 30 argue for creating clarity in a more directive way. People in operations, managers, project managers, are all inundated by the numerous priorities. In their opinion, the organization is considered unsafe; people don't know where they stand and what is expected of them. A plea for the top to truly take charge. These 30 speak of a crisis situation. They also emphasize the importance of the conversion of the measures and choices into instructions, tasks and objectives for individuals and groups: Disciplining as approach.

It is five to twelve. The Chairman expressly targets the two most important competitors. A picture of the enemy is created; a common enemy as a binder and catalyst. The Chairman combines it with a variant of 'fix it or sell it' with which Jack Welch has brought General Electric back on track. It is unfeasible to assess all businesses, projects and activities one by one by their content. Hence measures and targets are formulated that suit the requirement and the objective to beat the two most important competitors and take back the leading market position within a year.

Anne explains the nature and signification of this approach. "Dictating and Disciplining have been chosen. Inspiration has to come from being successful. We focus on defeating the enemy. This can result in considerable energy and solidarity. Think about Agincourt and the speech of Henry V. But such a mission and target also has its limitations. What about when the enemy is beaten? What do we do next? Moreover, it is a strong but negative motivation. That can come at a certain price, especially long term. The Chairman combines this form with a target mission. Concrete targets: leading market position, within a year. After that, we have and want to carry on!"

The draft is taking shape. A new change approach is needed. Imagining, with a renewed corporate story and collective ambition, seems to become the next phase. This will require more time than the first phase. It is essential to shape the ambition interactively and internalize it together. Image and engineering. The leadership will undergo an important accent shift. It is not only *one* activity, but also *everyone's* activity. The transition from the directive first phase to this second phase will require considerable effort. The phase is concluded with the further alignment of the strategy and structure with the new Rationale. The draft expresses that a probable next phase appears in which the approaches Fueling and Materializing play the main role. It is essential to shape desirability and feasibility proportionally. New energy is needed. In addition to new inspiration, it is also about the right people, financial possibilities, training and development. After that, the collective ambition has to be translated even further. What are the desired effects, which directives do we need to pursue? This is the introduction to the transition, from drastic changes to business as usual: from changing to running.

At the end of the third day, the leadership roles are the central point. What do we possess, what do we need? Do we have the Architects and Controllers to complete the first phase? Can we mobilize enough Storytellers, can they be developed? What must we do now in order to provide the leadership roles that are required for the third and fourth phase?

ONE YEAR LATER

The Chairman realizes that the change process with Anne has now been running for nearly a year. "Change is a profession," Anne often says, and it is clear by now that this statement is true. Tomorrow morning there will be an update with the works council, and this afternoon the Supervisory Board meeting. The Chairman will announce what the "interim score" is with regard to the change process. Since the new start with Anne, many things have taken place and a lot has been "successful" in the past two phases—a new language, a new way of looking. The first phase took the Chairman a lot of effort. The trajectory of the extensive diagnosis up to the change approach that Anne described as 'Dictation' took well over six months. It was followed by a subtle shift toward 'Disciplining' in that same first phase. That diagnosis was an experience in itself—confrontational, instructive and motivational.

That afternoon the meeting with the Supervisory Board went well. The first two phases have been carried out in accordance with the draft and with satisfactory results. The directors were impressed. Of course, they are curious about the next steps. The evaluation of the first phases has proven to be very instructive. The leading market position has been retaken. The second phase has produced a wonderful corporate story. The effort has also taken its toll. One member of the Board has left, several managers have moved on to somewhere else. The enemy mission is behind them, targets are not the mission now, but result from it. The new mission is all about the further transformation and setting the example, in every aspect. The next phase will literally and figuratively be fully invested in the capacity to realize the new ambitions. It is now crucial to persevere and hold on.

The Chairman has just called Anne. She was happy to hear the good news. Anne asked how he wanted to commence the next phase.

"Are you capable of addressing the crowd again with a personal story?" she asked the Chairman. "The previous Inspiring phase is now behind us. The effects are present. But that doesn't mean that the inspiring stops here. On the contrary. We are starting the transformation *now*. The strategic logic developed and the new business model are here, properly developed and invoked through the corporate story. But now it gets real. You are going to ask a lot from the organization and every individual."

"What should I do?" asked the Chairman.

"What do you have to *be*," says Anne.

"Well?"

Anne continued: "It is about the *why* of the change. The *what* and *how* are known and can be modeled on and after the subsequent phases. You have to stand for the coming change. Embody it!"

"That's what I want, indeed," says the Chairman, "but how do I realize that 'being' you are talking about?"

Anne asked: "Do you have examples of leaders you admire that were capable of incorporating the *why* of important change and expressing it?"

The Chairman thought about the work of psychologist Gardner and responded: "Thatcher and Gandhi."

"Wonderful classical examples, I think," Anne said. "Do you have a more recent but equally classic example?" asked Anne.

The Chairman thought about it. "ObamaCare!" he said. Anne waited. "Obama has taken his time to reform the health care in the United States. The Strategists and Controllers did their work very thoroughly before the presentation. Their plan was solid as a rock on both technical and analytical levels. The Storyteller and Framer still had to get through. Obama called the plan into existence during the presentation. He made clear *why* this reform was necessary. Explaining the essential point," says the Chairman.

"What appealed to you? What touched or moved you?" asks Anne.

"Wait a minute," the Chairman says. He looks in his computer and opens Obama's speech from 3 March 2010.

"Are you still there?" asked the Chairman to be sure, "I have found the quotes." He read to Anne:

> *"Today, I'm signing this reform bill into law on behalf of my mother, who argued with insurance companies even as she battled cancer in her final days. I'm signing it for Ryan Smith, who's here today. He runs a small business with five employees. He's trying to do the right thing, paying half the cost of coverage for his workers. This bill will help him afford that coverage. I'm signing it for 11-year-old Marcelas Owens, who's also here. Marcelas lost his mom to an illness. And she didn't have insurance and couldn't afford the care that she needed. So in her memory he has told her story across America so that no other children have to go through what his family has experienced. I'm signing it for Natoma Canfield. Natoma had to give up her health coverage after her rates were jacked up by more than 40 percent. She was terrified that an illness would mean she'd lose the house that her parents built, so she gave up her insurance. Now she's lying in a hospital bed, as we speak, faced with just such an illness, praying that she can somehow afford to get well without insurance. Natoma's family is here today because Natoma can't be. And her sister Connie is here. Connie, stand up. I'm signing this bill for all the leaders who took up this cause through the generations—from Teddy Roosevelt to Franklin Roosevelt, from Harry Truman, to Lyndon Johnson, from Bill and Hillary Clinton, to one of the deans who's been fighting this so long, John Dingell. To Senator Ted Kennedy. And it's fitting that Ted's widow, Vicki, is here and his niece Caroline; his son Patrick, whose vote helped make this reform a reality."[5]*

"The job is not nearly finished yet, but my job here is," Anne says. "Take care! Good night."

"Good night," the Chairman says and reflects on the discussion and Anne's last lesson.

NOTES

1. Sennett, R. (2008). *The craftsman.* New Haven, CT: Yale University Press.
2. Bauman, Z. (2001). *Community: Seeking safety in an insecure world.* Malden, MA: Blackwell Publishers.
3. Burger, Y., & Roos, A. (2011). Containment als voorwaarde voor leiderschapsontwikkeling. In J. Boonstra, J. Van Muijen & H. Tours (eds.), *Leiderschap in organisaties* (pp. 175–187). Deventer, NL: Kluwer.

4. Margolies, D. (2006). Henry V and ideology. In S. Hatchuel and N. Vienne-Guerrin (eds.), (2008), *Shakespeare on screen* (p. 149). Publications of the university of Rouen and Le Havre.
5. Remarks by President Obama and Vice President Biden at the signing of the Health Insurance Reform Bill (23 October 2010). Retrieved from http://www.whitehouse.gov/the-press-office/remarks-president-and-vice-president-signing-health-insurance-reform-bill.

Index

For Product Safety Concerns and Information please contact our EU
representative GPSR@taylorandfrancis.com
Taylor & Francis Verlag GmbH, Kaufingerstraße 24, 80331 München, Germany

www.ingramcontent.com/pod-product-compliance
Ingram Content Group UK Ltd.
Pitfield, Milton Keynes, MK11 3LW, UK
UKHW021609240425
457818UK00018B/458